The Taming of the Fork

Philip Golding

authorHOUSE®

AuthorHouse™ UK Ltd.
500 Avebury Boulevard
Central Milton Keynes, MK9 2BE
www.authorhouse.co.uk
Phone: 08001974150

First published by AuthorHouse 9/24/2008

ISBN: 978-1-4389-0037-7 (sc)

Printed in the United States of America
Bloomington, Indiana

This book is printed on acid-free paper.

Table of Contents

Forward
(March)

During your childhood years you work your way through the growing pains driving your parents mad. Having said that understanding all the rules and guidelines was no easy task. Still you get through all this with the add bruise but generally ok. The same can be said for your teenage years, but that had the fringe benefits loves first kiss. You move into adulthood get married and have your own children with their growing pains. Bosses at your office come and go but your career takes shape then life sneaks up behind you and scrambles the path you tread. Then to through you off course even further a 'curve ball' smacks you right in the kisser.

I got my 'curved ball in April 2005 when, after seeing my brilliant GP, Doctor McGawley. After spotting a tremor on a visit I went for some tests to confirm an 'involuntary tremor' or Parkinson's Disease. Guess which option won? When I was diagnosed it was like being dropped down a black hole, looking up and seeing your future disappearing to a tiny dot within your field of vision. This became the launch pad to 'boldly go where no where no member of my family had been before'. This 'new future' voyage I could not have contemplated without the love and support of my wife Jen and my two boys, Tom and Jack.

To have found my Parkinson's enabling rather than disabling, has surprised me. I have been down to the depths of despair and back. Somehow my condition has made me a 'richer' person by opening me to a new world of possibilities. After all how do you know what is behind a door unless you try the handle? I feel incredibly lucky to have my immediate and extended family supporting me. Without them, my friends and work mates I wouldn't have written this forward and you would not be reading my first book of poetry.

As I have written my poems I got to think about how society views me and other disabled people. How could I help others understand how a disabled person feels, who lives life to the max, and has the same right to access all levels in this society? How could I put back some of the benefits that I have gratefully received? That is when I wrote my first poem 'The Taming of the Fork', one sleepless night on holiday with close friends of ours in Ilfracoombe.

That poem was the key that opened up the sluice gates holding back my creativity.

I have written over 250 poems since that fateful date in Ilfracoombe. In my Parkinson's world I am not in control, but in the world where my words create pictures, I am in charge. IT helps me attempt to make sense of my ever changing world. Sometimes I write about Parkinson's in a semi-serious way. I find humour can take the edge of my condition. Poetry is a two way gateway between writer and audience as I have discovered since I have become a performance poet.

Whether you are able bodied or disabled these written offerings will provoke an array of emotions and mix them all up then place it in a pocket of your heart. If I end up helping just one reader with my poems then all the many hours spent on my laptop computer will have been a success.

Welcome to my world betwixt these sheets.

The Taming of the Fork

Both my hands have been there for me all my life
Putting food in my mouth using fork and knife
Any job given to them they found easy to handle
Lifting a heavy weight or lighting delicate candle

Any job needed requiring my hands I only had to ask
Each of my hands, eager to please they rose to the task
Over the years my left hand grew jealous of the right
Lefty never forgave brain for not being chosen to write

A campaign plotting revenge lefty he began planning
Disrupting brains system used for message handling
Lefty worked hard on precise plans for his campaign
To wreak havoc and end his being controlled by brain

Lefty, he became bitter, twisted and rotten to the core
The military plan's completed, he made for brains door
Lefty's pent up bitterness would finally come to an end
Blocking the lines for the messages that brain did send

A long campaign finally breeched the brain owners' door
He was diagnosed with Parkinson's at aged forty-four
His left hand trembled, he stuttered when trying to talk
He shuffled his feet and couldn't even turn his fork

Brain started its heroic fight with a rearguard action
Sought outside alliances and formed a military faction
Developing a series of weapons brain found a super drug
To repair communication lines and a system to de-bug

With some initial successes lefty is being forced back
Brains control returning when lefty mounts an attack
The battle with the fork is but one within a bigger war
Subsequent conflicts joined, fought and levelling the score

Through each battle Brains confidence, it comes and it goes
New weaponry sometimes needed to vanquish all his foes
A treaty is being discussed by Brain and lefty at the table
As for the taming of the fork, that task is now most stable

Doctors, what do they know?

I have been diagnosed with Parkinson's by the doctors, but I feel ok
Should I really listen to their pronouncement or to anything they say
Surely I should know my own body; all of its multiple-interactions
Doctors, what do they know? I don't require their kind of sanctions.

So, they have studied for a few years and may be passed a few exams
I bet half those who diagnosed me have only just left their own prams
Have not I been the one to look after my mind and body all my life?
We have gone through thick and thin without much by way of strife

Like most people I get the odd sniffle maybe even a recurrent sneeze
All these common bugs everyone gets are blown away in the breeze
Sure I have a stutter, an odd shuffle and even an occasional tremor
What to do about it? I'm not too sure, isn't it just another dilemma

Should I accept help from these doctors or specialist within the NHS?
They seem to know their subject and sort of ok with the odd diagnosis
My confidence is waning; I am not sure what I should do from now
I think that perhaps now it is time to listen, take it on board some how

My doctor was thoroughly helpful sat me down and was there to listen
She went through it all using my language, it didn't become a lesson
I had some tests, and from there, referred onto a Parkinson's specialist
He diagnosed me when I was 44; re the condition he was the optimist

My specialist, he gave reasons my ailments both verbally and written
It was my turn to take on board the advice, with its content, not smitten
Do I need medical help or any of the drug regimes said to need, do I
I could cope with diagnosis, heeding my own council on it, couldn't I?

Six months after my diagnosis I couldn't, my coping had gone to pot
Confidence in my abilities at work and home was fine though err not
I went to see my doctor who referred my cry for help onto my specialist
My drug regime my safety put in place, he remained ever the optimist

It was for me like an admission that Parkinson's existed and very real
I was now at the lowest point my persona with a distinct lack of zeal
Medically, I had my turning point a platform on which I could build
I have my support network around me a protective and valiant shield

Six Rings for an Answer Machine!

There is a ring of soapsuds left around the bath thrown up by the waves created as I bathe. I had received my diagnosis today. Psychologically I was washing the disease from me. As do onshore waves rid the sea of the unwanted flotsam onto the beach at high water mark.

There is a ring of fate determined that I should have developed Parkinson's. I seem to attract problems'; it must be my magnetic personality. Just when things seem to be going well I get something else thrown at me or I resolve issues then there is a twist in the plot. Well, the plot stinks. Why should I be in a position where I am trying to climb a down escalator in order to the next floor? Just as I get to the next step there is another and another. Sometimes you get tired of fighting back and, well you can surmise the rest. Well I'm sick of this? Nobody in my family has developed Parkinson's, lucky me.

There is a ring of change is resounding. I look around, distracted once again from my goal to find out what the fuss is about. Am I to be redirected, seemingly? All this appears to be like a maze made from coins stacked high, entitled 'The Circle of Life'. A mouse is placed in the centre and left to find their way out. Mouse sniffs a way out and begins inching his way along, when suddenly coins topple forcing it to stop and re-evaluate. I am that mouse and you can toss that coin again, "Heads". I deserve a change in fortune.

There is a ring of truth dawning as I sit on my imaginary hillside watching the sunrise, listening the bird song on the air. I sometimes go there, a place only I know, to get me out of the 'rat race' for a while. It helps me try to make sense of my problems. This Parkinson's Disease set of issues is huge to come to terms with. It has taken me eighteen months of going to my hillside being warmed by the sun and wafted by a gentle summer breeze coming up to me from the meadow below. I have just accepted the truth about having developed my condition, but it's a bitter pill to swallow, several.

There is a ring of confidence building up inside me, giving me hope. The cards I have been dealt might not be the best, but I steadily learn how to play them. My cards help, increasingly, to develop my hand each round steering me towards my objectives. Not every card will be kind to me when it comes to me from the Parkinson's deck. I do know I can draw from other decks to bolster my cards each round. My wife, family, friends and Doctor's help me deal with my condition. I can't lose, can I?

There is the sixth ring, pick up the phone, and come on. I know I'm a bit over enthusiastic, but I hope they can offer an answer to my ultimate question, 'Is there something that can eradicate Parkinson's from my system, now, so that I can lead the life I had wanted?' Great they have picked up the phone, "Hello," I was

"There is nobody to take you're call right now we're trying to find a cure. So if you would like to leave your name and number after this tone a Consultant will get back to you" beeeeeeeeeeeep!

Bugger!!

Curved Balls

'Curved Balls' of life come at you from all angles and serve to confuse
When the meteoric Parkinson's ball hit, its onslaught I couldn't refuse
What had once been firmly built foundations had dissolved into mud
There was me scrabbling around on the ground salvaging what I could
Since I came to terms with my disease and started writing my poetry
It never ceases to surprise me the number of windows of opportunity
Yes I have my pain, discomfort, lack of control and I want my cure now
But, for every minus there is a plus, even with Parkinson's somehow
Up to October 2005 I had a lot of rubbish swirling around in my head
Then on holiday one wakeful night I wrote my first poem, sat up in bed
This opened gates holding back my complex feelings bringing them in line
Poems just flooded out, enough a book? Was somebody giving a sign?
Now I've enough for three, ideas for books, written 2 songs and a hymn
This Parkinson's has unleashed a writer. Fame! Chances are at best, slim
What this has done is provide focus for me and has straighten my mind
What has helped me come to terms with my disease I give to you in kind?
So, if you are sat, stood, or lying down reading me I give you this thought
What baggage have you had to deal with? Barraged with things to seek!
My advice to you get yourself to a PC and type. Use a pen, papers speak
Release those pent up confusing thoughts helps get them straight instead.
All got me straighter, opening up chances, though I still moments stressed
Whenever confidence drains from me? What to do? Yes you've guessed
The how's, when's, what's for writing aren't vital. Self-help is the point.
You're in control of this world and let your troubles with your words anoint.

Son of Parkin

Reading my disease title for the first time after diagnosis got me thinking just who was this 'Parkin' and more importantly who was his son. So I decided in my mind to speculate hypothetically the origin of their name and its use today.

Did the name come from yester year when God was handing people their names out. The Lord had said that each person's name must befit his allocated task for which he had been placed on the Earth. Anyway it was late in the day and the queue for names had been long. The Lord was getting tired, worn out and wanted a bath. He saw this chap coming for his name and thought he would call in his opposite side, a Mr D'vil, took look after this poor chap.

This sickly looking gent had reached the front of the queue, just before closing time, and Mr D'vil looked at him squarely in the eyes. Deep into his sole he saw, a blackened heart, which lit up a mischievous glow in him. He thought this wirery guy could work for me bringing pain and suffering to millions. So he put it to this man that he had been having few problems outside his establishment with carrier drivers pulling in with a name on the side of Carter. This sickly chap, with blackened heart, was put to work and given a name that reflected his profession, Parkin.

So it was on that unfortunate day that the profession hated throughout the world first came to pass outside Mr D'vils establishment. Over the years he's had many children, mainly boys, each with a heart similarly afflicted. These Sons of Parkin live on today still possessing that curse from Mr D'vil. They plague our lives across the land. Who are these people so loathed to be cursed so roundly each day?

What was the job Parkin and then his son given? Why it was 'Traffic Warden'.

I've Joined the Famous

Who would have thought it that one day that I'd be in the hall of fame
Sharing the stage, facing crowds next to the evangelist Billy Graham
Or join Pope John Paul the second talking to millions performing mass
Two illustrious religious leaders, reaching out, that's what I call class

President Harry Truman, Fidel Castro, even Chairman Mao Tse Tung
Who would have thought it? My self-esteem has gone up another rung
It was nice of them to join me to share my journey to fame and glory
I'd tell you all about it but not within a poem, it is a full-blown story

I am leading thespian standing in naught but grease paint and socks
Supported by Katherine Hepburn, Terry Thomas, and Michael J Fox.
Top billing Actors, who made me laugh and cry within their profession
Life is but a play to be reviewed, it can be scary that is my confession

To ward off any bad reviewers we all need our defender and our ally
Who would better to have on your team than boxer Mohammad Ali?
You are Commander in Chief, fighting your own demons out there
To advise you on your tactics who better than General Macarthur

We all have our champions supporting our trials and tribulations
Family and friends have become our very own 'United Nations'
So whether your condition developed early or was it shown late on
Use the power of words retrieve 'inner you', read poet Irvine Layton

Richer, Tomorrow

For that richer tomorrow
I had only planned it yesterday
There, it lies, fragmented
Desolate in the hallway of my mind
That blue print, MY blue print
Ground into the carpets weave
As if 'worked over' by an industrial vacuum cleaner
Parts flake off, my future floats away
Like the ashes from a burning fire
They say I've got an involuntary tremor
Or this Parkinson's gig
Why me WHY MEeeeeeee!
I've got a wonderful wife
She doesn't deserve all this
And my boys, MY BOYS
They are only young
They don't want a dad
On meds destined for a wheelchair
Fingers crossed for tremor

I went to see this specialist today.
'One more test for you, Mr Golding'
BASTARDS, I'VE GOT PARKISON'S
That's it life over, totally screwed
Why couldn't you tell me four years ago?
When I started putting my family through it
Started four long years of study
For a degree I can't use
My future, a huge metal climbing frame
Twisted into impossible shapes
Fashioned by this, this jug-naught thing!
Why me God?
Why couldn't the truck turned off earlier
Instead of me being up the junction
My whole LIFE is down the pan

My plan, My plan
My ....flush

Dawns first awakenings rush into my mind
In the hallway of my mind sits my phone
The green answering machine light flashed
On off, on off, on off ON
Was I actually dreaming?
Pressed the listen button, eh
"This is deep thought", this voice said,
"We have come up with a plan".
I splashed cold water on my face
Starred at this bloke in the mirror
Then my face light like a 200watt light bulb
YES, if I just do this, tweak that
I HAD a plan, I can achieve, I will achieve
That metal frame is forged anew
Got myself a new flexible enabling plan
Got choice, got my goals
Parky will always be nipping at my heals
But for now Parky mate,
I'm in charge
Its two fingers to you.

Weapons of Mass Construction

The body's edifice is a superb machine guarded by a military might
Delivering many blows against all foes's chucking them out of sight
Many a recruit cells pass through 'Boot Camp' marching in the rain
They undergo all groundwork under the guidance of Sergeant Brain

A bigwig, turned renegade from Whitehall, threatens its very success
Sending confusing memos leaving all communication lines a mess
The medical section, however, have solutions to reorganize and de-bug
Doctors, family plus supporting network along with many a drug

Initial diagnostics were executed my team of doctors and consultants
Sliding in recruits Ropinerol and Selegilene as 'Boot Camp' occupants
With regular use they brought communication systems back on line
For several months the training camp had its weapons doing just fine

Whitehall got wind of this noticing the camps budgetary overspend
They sent in their own team of consultants to bring this era to an end
Disrupting the new recruits by when they were taken and their effect
Depression, Anxiety, and Confidence, could they cause drugs to eject?

Throughout this power struggle my network of friends all support me
By them listening to my explanations they in turn help wonderfully
My medical team have new boy Sinimet and their stance is proactive
More networks and physio switch my life into being more constructive

Occasionally I have forgotten to take my tablets or at the wrong time
To do this to my system even after all their advice is far from sublime
Taking medicines regularly each day, accepting help is my deduction
Means you're not alone and you posses 'Weapons of Mass Construction'

It's Not Just Me

When my brain of mine started to malfunction
The doctors found a label for my chemical soup
Parkinson's it read, which initially didn't dawn
It's not just me who has unjustly been afflicted

Sometimes when I am alone with my thoughts
They wander from the man I was to him I'm going to be
Waves of sadness envelope me, overcome senses
I sob uncontrollably into a dark place devoid of reason

The love of my life had married me for me myself
She hadn't married this chemically modified future me
This was our voyage of discovery our all time love
I want her for my wife, my lover not as my carer

God blessed our love with two wonderful boys
They had every right to expect an energetic dad
I was supposed to be a fun, dad a perfect role model
I was supposed to care for them, not them me

As a son of my parents love, I was the next generation
Don't son's grow up, leave home, testimony to their love
Shouldn't they sit back with satisfaction as I achieved
They should've had their retirement, not worry over me

As my Parkinson's creeps over me, overtaking systems
I worry what my friends see when face muscles stiffen
Do they think me boring person when my look so serious
Fatigue slows me down, I get tired, but I'm still me

I sometime panic wondering what strangers see
If I need a stick that immediately I am ten years older
As I walk; I shuffle, stagger along a sober drunk
I've seen those looks saying 'look at that piss head'

I still weep in the dark, but sometimes I get stubborn
I get real angry thinking the degree I got was wasted
Then I say be dammed with all my Parkinsonism
I have a lot to offer and by God the world will get it

From Sneeze to Disease FX

From my diagnosis there have been plenty of times for reflection
Where had this disease originate from and why in my direction?
There hadn't been any family history of Parkinson's on either side
Why had my life become overrun by this poisonous crimson tide?

Like a tiny note wanting to be heard amidst an orchestral piece
I struggled to find where I could pitch 'why' and confusion cease
I was trying to take in explanations from the internet and or book
Becoming overwhelmed I 'lost the plot' not knowing where to look

By chance I was reading an article about sufferers from hay fever
How lifelong sufferers can develop Parkinson's, I'm now a believer
From an early age I took stronger and stronger tablets and spays
The older I got my body grew less reliant on them in many ways

I was within that small percentage of hay fever sufferers, lucky me
It did, however, clear the mists of confusion clearing the mystery
Having my 'why and where' solved it gave a kind of recompense
A payment for the research and brought an insight to my parents

Both theirs and my mind had struck out trying to apportion blame
How from an ember called 'Hay fever' came the 'Parkinson flame'
I went into freefall my world blackened by the unbearable heat
My choice was, whether to try and regain life or a certain defeat

All this medication I take to keep control, what future it paints
I take nineteen a day at going to print, are there any restraints
It's a battle for control as new symptoms rears their ugly head
The doctors scratch their chin, send in pills and knock it dead

The symptoms creep up on you like guerrillas shrouded by mist
Playing tricks on your body making it ache, stumble and twist
Movie directors and stuntmen would kill for action you can pull
Only another suffer of the disease can be Parkinson's stunt double

Our involuntary acting skills are restrained by operations or pills
They leave the audience bemused or running away up the hills
I may not get a part in a Hollywood blockbuster, they're not rife
But I choose the biggest and toughest role, I choose live my life

Naff Day

Absolutely naff day
Needed a laugh day
Suffer lack of sleep day
Upset along the way day
Demands from all sides day
Parkinson's play day
Ached all day
Even take a Monday
Next week holiday
Turn other cheek week
Everything Greek week
Back Tuesday week
Going to be a great week
Recharged batteries week
Then talk to friend's week
Be more refined week
Down bottle wine week
Inspired again week
Old me back week

The Best Form of Defence is Attack

I was walking in the park on day enjoying the wide-open space. The warm summer breeze wafted gently through the trees. The swallows were flitting high in the hazy blue sky. Mums and Dads were playing with their children or queuing for an ice cream. Ambling gently as I was in no rush I saw a squirrel dart up a tree via a bush.

My feet started to feel strange, a slight heat inside my feet; they stopped and started tripping me of their own accord. Half falling I looked down seeking an answer to whether my laces had come undone. My legs joined in the assault and I started staggering about like the town drunk, only sober. What being had visited this upon me placing these varying invisible barriers? Then there's me trying the jump over them like the fences in the 'Grand National'?

The light-hearted feeling brought on by the blue skies had turned to grey. The storm clouds of embarrassment were forming as people turned their heads to stare. Fences grew around me. I felt segregated, isolated and alone. Why was this happening to me? Just who had I upset? WHY? WHY? WHY?

My eyes began to open, slowly at first, I was afraid of what I might see surrounding me. I felt the sheets wrapped tightly around me. Untangling myself I felt pain in my legs, my right foot was on fire. My hand was now shaking wildly. Had my body been swapped overnight? Had my brain taken flight with those swallows? Help me what should I do? Was the life that I knew over? Should I pack up? Noooooooooooooooooooooooooo.

After getting dressed I was onto my doctors. At my appointment she said it was either an involuntary tremor or Parkinson's. I felt as though I had been smacked in the face by a wet fish. That's it curtains down. She explained it all, which helped me calm down. I was referred onto a specialist to check me out. Please don't confirm, please don't confirm – he did. I was diagnosed with Parkinson's at 44.

Whilst denying it all I was slipping down this chasm of denial and despair. I was disappearing into a black hole. As I fell my eye caught a chink of light a short distance below. With the last of my metal strength I struck out with my arm into the blackness and my hand caught a vine like root. My direction was changing, drifting towards the light. I caught hold of the ledge and hauled myself up. I sat there momentarily contemplating whether to continue down or press on towards the light. How was I going to cope? What was my strategy? How would I climb over this psychological barrier, this six-foot fence? Did I have the strength to get myself back to my dream park, enjoying that summer breeze and sip a cool glass of wine?

Just show me the light and watch me go. I am going to get that control back. My destiny is in my hands. Sure I have got Parkinson's but I still decide how I play the life cards I have been dealt. I can choose. Fences are made of wood and wood makes for a great set of steps. Steps lead onto platforms, a solid base on which to build my future and with the support that's always going to be there for me.

Welcome back the real me. Though it's taken along time to come to terms with my Parkinson's it is true that the best form of d'fence is attack.

"White wine please".

Choicest Cuts

Choicest cuts in the life I had, gone
Choices that I thought were mine
Choices faded into the depressive mists of time
Choices wrenched from weakening grip
Choices in my ability to something, like speech issues, frustrate
Choices in being who I wanted to be, seem blocked
Choices, in summing up for me, are now history

Parkinson's wasn't my choice?
Losing my sense of smell wasn't my choice
Not being allowed to drive due to medication not my choice
Having an obsessive compulsive disorder wasn't my choice
Starting conversations with hallucinations wasn't my choice
Forgetting how to walk or staggering in the street, not my choice
Having a short term memory problem wasn't my choices

Then again I chose to write these verses you read
Then again through my writing I have made new friends
Then again I can help others cope with my disability
Then again I can self-help, by writing down issues bothering me
Then again I can still perform on stage to exercise my throat
Then again I can still enable parts of society understand
Then again I can still show the world that I'm still here, **it's me!**

Feel Pride
(Based around the signature tune 'Raw Hide)

Parkinson's in me is stirring
Parkinson's in me is stirring
Parkinson's in me is stirring

Parkinson's in me is stirring
See my body popping
Keep those tablets coming?
Turn the tide
Trip, fall, or stammer
For my future I clamber
With my Jen by my side
All her love and kissin'
We've always sailed with the tide
She's my rock can't be denied

Take a pill (swallow down)
Physio (walk around)
Parky nurse (turn around)
Feel Pride
Take a pill (swallow down)
Physio (walk around)
Parky nurse (turn around)
Feel Pride

Just keep your body moving
Though it sometimes is stumbling
Keep your body moving?
Feel Pride

Try to understand this disease
This cure continues to tease
This condition brings me to my knees

Find a way forward; turn the keys
The will come though not with ease
Just press forward if you please

Take a pill (swallow down)
Physio (walk around)
Parky nurse (turn around)
Feel Pride
Take a pill (swallow down)
Physio (walk around)
Parky nurse (turn around)
Feel Pride

Feel pride
Oh yes
Parkinson's in me is stirring
Parkinson's in me is stirring
Oh yes
Parkinson's in me is stirring
Parkinson's in me is stirring
Feel Pride

Deep-Rest

Today I have felt quite out of sorts; never quite got going; heavy eyes
I have been depressed; felt isolated; I sit here longing yesteryear highs
Maybe I should drink a hot chocolaty drink or just sniff some chloroform
Only had three hours kip last night I wish seven would become the norm

It would be great to relive dreams of adventure; even I can be a superhero
Rather than climb out bed; be wide awake at three a.m.; feel like a super-zero
My walking-gate was bad today; I was walking around flippers on my feet!
Perhaps someone should have thrown me a fish, balance a ball; fall on my seat

Today I have been like a bear with a sore head; perhaps I should see the vet
I should have gone back to bed; spent all day to get a deep rest, under a duvet
Sailing along the Parkinson Sea has not been smooth in fact it was quite choppy
Stupid me was sat beneath the deck the steering wheel tied; knots rather sloppy

The whole day has been like a poor 'B' movie, watched on a pirate copy DVD
With me as the 'Z' actor with no chance of an 'Oscar', or small part in repartee
I need to talk to someone, get this madness out, or drink beer from a glass
Sit down for a while, read a book, take the load off my feet or fall on my ass

A few times I've had to repeat myself, Parkinson's given poor me enunciation
It's feels awkward, I can hear me, still I repeat with slowed down articulation
I am now back at home just wandering in a random fashion from room to room
Trying to find anything to focus on trying to escape my mood, a dark grey plume

My breathing felt laboured as if constricted by some torturous straight jacket
The way I perceive things to have been, it's the funny farm but it'd cost a packet
Every time I tried to speak to my wife there were a million and one interruptions
I had to walk away, give up trying to explain or risk some volcanic eruptions

Finally I emerge from my cocoon at 9pm much to mine and everybody's relief
The grey clouds had finally been dispersed out came the bright sunshine of belief
To secure 'my little ray of sunshine' I had to write, put this poetry into motion
The sun is so high in the sky, bringing warmth; I need a factor 40 sun tan lotion

Now the 'being depressed' has been routed and all that's wrong down on paper
I will have my chocolaty drink, not chloroform, up to bed as fast as I can caper
Take a long hot bath, relax, read a book, but above all get a very deep rest
Wake up next morning, with a mild suntan, feeling jolly and heavenly blest

To be or not to be?

To be or not to be, a Parkinson's question:
Only for lack of Dopamine wouldst mind suffer.
Hand shakes across virgin page,
Or should I use quill or nib to calm waves of indecision,
And the frustration? To cry: to scream;
That's it; the quill; by choosing this tool, will this be the end?
The anxiety and agony of sufferers' painful choice;
To control my movement, 'tis the objective
Directing myself? I wish, as I sleep;
To dream of my renewed world: dare I hope;
Within dreams of a regaining control; what imaginations come?
When my mind shuffles about the field of faltering controls;
Memory's flicker and die; Memory I should expect.
Sufferers can be tied up betwixt feelings of rejection and respect, forever;
Could rejection be accepted over this life, a life in freefall?
These torments and erosion fraught by chemical imbalances; old me steadily
is so consumed,
Fear no more the frown of a doctor's brow.
Forget not, their influence will enhance your movements. Our patient
endeavour rewards undiscovered country, to gain motion; further acclaim;
Lay bare the thorns of Parkinson's onset.
The desire to strive forth, knowing ambitions remain, bourn from past
honest toil, halts my stride and I look back in awe.
May cause me to pause and cry. Oh! Such wonder in past dreams.
Was the Lord not aware of my long nights deciding careers choice, my ambition?
Now spent, trying to reconnect or bi-pass communication lines, that dust
seem sometimes cause lost.
How I dust tear out my hair, mutter and swear;
Such is the torment of a Parkinson's suffers life. The all consuming fear that
I may be
Abandoned like a book on a dark dusty shelf, like an
Undiscovered manuscript that's lost to outrageous fortune.
Oh! The angst; the calumny of no self will.
The course down which future will flow is as unclear,
as a 'Droplet of water racing down yonder window pain'.

But, 'Hold', do not be so engaged with such vagueness, listen to audience applaud my Parkinson's disease poetry. Fly to their counsel; embrace their office o'er and o'er. Layers of creativity burst forth from this mortal coil, as the first flower of spring bursting from winter's bosom. Butterfly's flutter within, as ink tipped quill gently caresses the untouched page, now flavoured by creative actions. Perchance I may create a 'Painting of Words' for you. Perchance for you, like me, such tensions through writings may find release.

A tapestry, to will kingdoms to embrace uncharted seas;
For if choice for sufferers is to be or not to be? I choose 'to be'.

I Live in a Space Ship

I am the urban spaceship watch me fly, my space is around up to the sky
From the outside I wobble and stumble, sometimes my shake and fumble
Within its still me running around inside, the things going on, what pride
It's like a whole different universe totally free, when I'm controlling me
Sometimes I look all normal from the outside; I'm hiding from hell inside
Then again the gift of humour bursting out, plus superb ideas with clout
I'm not interested in just being labelled, some poor unfortunate disabled
My Parky's fuel rods have knocked directional trim, this ship's on a whim
I've got these power pills to dilute the effect, my lives not quite wrecked
This spaceship is now moving on a different plain, a twisting tilting train
Poems, policy reports, children's stories, they keep coming out in flurries
So no matter what's happening to me, even better is coming, definitely

Changes in Me

From the time I came into this world images and experiences have invaded my being, absorbed as quickly as water being soaked up by a dry sponge. Each vision came its set of instructions are just like my own overworked parliamentarian not sure which policy is going to work best. Whilst trying to make sense of these new experiences that brought uninvited changes in me.

These changes have spawned another and another as if sending me up in a remote control warplane called 'Confusion' being scrambled to fight an imaginary foe. Just who is being scrambled? Is the air traffic controller having a laugh at my expense or trying to guide me? I wish he would make his mind up for each change in altitude has brought about spiralling changes in me.

Growing up you try to be independent but find you always need or have to rely on others. Each then becomes a momentary partner in your stages of development. It's a bit like 'speed dating', you have got three minutes to get to know your next self before a whistle is blown and you have to move on. Sometimes I feel safe with my next self. Sometimes I'd like to ram that whistle down the host's throat, as I'd like to get to know my new self that has brought these individual changes in me.

Just whom do I need to please to win approval of choices I make? Have I entered some inventor's competition and I sit there eagerly awaiting these under qualified judges. I smile and demonstrate my system, my invention in the vain hope they can grasp its concept. They pass again. I don't get my award again this year, never mind. Hey, hang on a minute, that system does work and it pleases me that it brought directional changes in me.

You can lead a horse to water they say, but just what motivates it to drink? My body is like a stubborn mule with its own mind on directional movements. I kick its flanks and pull on its reigns, but the head just turns and the eye gives me that look. No chance mate! As its owner, not just a stable mate, I have incentives to spur me on. I have a team of trainers working for me. Don't reign in, keep up with or go ahead of others. I am motivated and enabled to bring about galloping changes in me.

It's a battle for to keep ahead of the game with parts of me breaking down. Cells of resistance are breaking down turning into a castle ruin. I try to rebuild fortifications, but the enemy is too strong. During a lull in the engagements I sit there, motionless, staring at a mirror a face devoid of emotion. Then along comes a twist of fate changing me from battle weary. Chinks within my foes armour appear as if pierced by my last arrows. I find the strength from somewhere to enable me to soldier on and bring about crusading changes in me.

Take the 'Dis' out of Disable

Through the tapestry of life we see types disability set out at the table
It makes me mad; who do they think they are. Do I really need a label?
No matter what outer signs or symptoms I show I am still full of pride
Look into my eyes listen to my voice I am still the same person inside

They say that you should deal with the cards you've got in your deck
I had to shout 'twist' and out came the Parkinson's card, wait just a sec
Who put that card in there when some cruel twist of fate has let it out?
I did not want that card I say but 'those are the rules' to me you shout

The way I interpret my new deck of cards will still facilitate any choice
Choosing cards expands my alternatives, helping others to hear my voice
The thing that alters is the type of surface on which I play not the team
I still have plans and goals that are my project to illustrate my dream

Just because I am classed as disabled don't you position me in a corner?
Please don't treat me the same as the nursery rhyme 'Little Jack Horner'
All my skills and attributes are there for me to use and are not a fable
Look at me and please take the 'dis' out of me for what you get is 'able'

Shun the Disease

When it all started between me and this disease I put a partition
I tried to turn away each time the doctors tried to give their rendition
Not wanting to hear the truth behind what wasn't any of my volition
When I received such, the news I felt it ended my world's continuation
All that I had taken for granted had now ceased to exist as one nation
Some plans disappeared or altered drastically got a feeling of deprivation
News of my Parkinson's seeped through the cracks ended my emancipation
I needed to reshape, crafting new plans that would work with my situation
Goals reset and, working with my family and friends they'd been consultation

My family helped reset goals, taught other friends and refreshed me

Consultation with other had helped me teach and be taught, refreshed my goals
Situation after situation transformed, I believe I can make my mark, can't I
Emancipation of my self released through the cracks, a Parkinson Key news
Deprivation levels dropped my vision rep-affirmed, re-crafted and then some
Nation as one! Well maybe not quite, a nation with new partners describes it all
Continuation with the news hour headlines always changed since way back when
Volition yes there are always options its better have exercised choice than not
Rendition describes a version of what they express, but in the end its down to I
Partition can be a sweet sorrow, what I do with the disease isn't an if it's a when

Letter to a Psychic

Dear Claire Voyant,

I am writing to you with regards to a visit my wife and I made to your establishment. We were the couple that were very sceptical and treated it as a joke, but things change.

The prediction you gave stated that we would end up on some top named show where we would meet the actor Russell Crow. We have always enjoyed chat shows and felt confident your prediction would come through. The next day we were talking about it, as we sat in a waiting room in our hospital for my test results.

Your prediction was correct I was going to see Parkinson, the disease not the show. I still had my special guest, no not Russell, Dr Clouseau. I feel I ought to complain to Blackpool Council re your prediction as the joke is now on me. Are your tarot cards not a full deck? Has your crystal ball bounced one too many times?

But in reality I would like to thank you, as I had been unemployed for some time. Since our visit I have managed to get a few jobs. My present vocation is as a 'Cocktail Shaker'. This has become easy money and has enabled me to buy out my previous employer. This tremor of mine has been an absolute godsend. This traumatic turn of events is, I think, beyond any medium.

Inadvertently you gave me a key, a key that has opened a bright and colourful future for me. I have my pot of gold from to the end of the rainbow. Once again thank you.

Yours sincerely,

Roy Gbiv

Passionate Parkinson's Predicts

This "Passionate Parkinson's Preacher Predicts Problems Pass"
Can only be said by a 'Shakespearian Actor' sipping water, alas
The feat accomplished whilst they are perched on their two big toes
With umbrellas as protection for the audience on the front two rows

His sermons were delivered to the converted in wit, verse and pros
Some were both dull and lengthy making listeners nod and dose
The topics weren't known to be restricted, the message there to imitate
There meaning was aired with dignity leaving an Image to emulate

His delivery wasn't always in a church or wearing perceived dress code
He once stood on the back of a horse as through the village it strode
What was said about Parkinson's was passionate, came from the heart
The horse looked up caught sight of what he's wearing, gave it a start

Although what came across in the sermon it hit home, struck a cord
Thanks to that horse his very next sermon came from a hospital ward
All his treatments I forgot to mention gave him bad water retention
He was cured with a few kind words via a pole with a 10 ft extension

He left the hospital and onto to a correctional institution with little rule
Dressed in tee shirt and jeans he thought he must look to be oh so cool
He delivered his next lecture but it all ended up back on a stretcher
His words reached out to a few, saw him as a teacher not a preacher

Back on the same ward and hospital he brought the barriers down
Unfortunately on his head whilst wearing his dressing gown
With broken bones and contusions but let there be no confusion
Communication lines are clear and open let there be no illusion

Even though he's been ordered to rest whilst he is taking a sabbatical
On the subject of Parkinson's our preacher is still just as fanatical
He has discovered Young Parkinson's Network and formed a class
Brought many sufferers together said with help problems can pass

At the end of his preaching life on the condition he is still sentimental
Just who's going to spread the message, take on that Parkinson Mantle?
The institution he'd visited all those years ago where he'd reached a few
He'd passed on his passion about Parkinson's now I pass it over to you

Sometimes

Sometimes when I'm in bed at night with a pain that's so sharp I can feel the needles goings in like a voodoo doll was modelled on me.

Sometimes it's like parliamentary question time in my head, debating with 'him upstairs' on why my body was awarded the 'Parkinson's Contract', despite stiff competition.

Sometimes I am 'over tired' warn out by the simplest of tasks, which once I took for granted. When I was a boy they said 'eat all your food and you'll grow up to be a big strong boy'. Well, I'm all grown up, just who got my strength?

Sometimes I reflect on my life, what it was, what it is now and yet to be? I tie myself in so many knots it's like spaghetti junction having a bad hair day. You can never quite straighten things out before another set of traffic comes down life's motorway.

Sometimes do I kid myself that I have fully come to terms with my uninvited guest? Who put him in charge? Why should I accept these new terms of my condition? When was I consulted? Can't I just throw them out as you would any garbage? I was here first.

Sometimes when I look at my wife and two boys I think what have they done so wrong? They have their own futures. They have to experience life, not to be restricted by a father who they may well need to look after. Though, I know they will always be there for me as my supporting foundation.

Sometimes I get the mental strength to deal with the cards I have. They may not be a 'Royal Flush', but I can still play a few tricks. I debate my personal issues with my peers in an imaginary council chamber. Even in my authority decisions are reached!

Sometimes my true self peeks out, just long enough to be noticed. I try to force 'self' out from behind that psychological barrier. It helps me do that when I can help others. On occasion I get great success, on others 'self' slips away under the cover of darkness. My condition makes life one big 'roller coaster'.

Sometimes my frustration spills out like two drunks being thrown out of a pub for fighting only to carry it on outside. The pain; anxiety; lack of confidence. I just want to SWEAR LOUDLY...@$%*><^#~ there that's better.

Sometimes I am in the right place at the right time where I can still be that rock on which there is still a strong foundation. My Parkinson's becomes my way in to help my friends and family understand. I want to help others with disabilities, focusing on what they have to offer, helping them to realize they can decide their future. Doctor heal thyself.

Sometimes I now realize that there is reason why I am who I am and why I have been sent down this road? My project in life is to help empower others, a target I accept. I believe we have are our own 'Superhero' within us. Superhero's always have their own sidekick when help is needed. I picked the best; I married 'Occupational Therapy Woman!'

Bouncing Back and Forth

My soul is a seaming cricket ball
Hit for runs towards the boundary
I'm stumped 'how's that' you call
Life isn't a mould made in a foundry

My life is like a game of table tennis
Will I be pinged or will I be ponged
Sometimes problems can be a mennis
Hitting a smash into a future I belonged

My life has the roundness and strength of a car tire
Treading carefully; bouncing on uneven road
Seeking the solutions when circumstances conspire
Support from all with a wide and heavy load

My life can be like a fortnight at Wimbledon
An expensive bowl of strawberries and cream
I'll serve for the set as interferers rambled on
Life is not a bowl of cherries but I'll still dream

My life's is contained within a boxing ring I've found
Punching my opponents to gain the upper hand
Bouncing back and forth until champ I am crowned
Be sure my Parkinson's my future is still planned

Raise the Barrier

We have to surmount many barriers with each new day we face
Trying to get past or over them; sometimes forced to re-trace
Everyone is trying to get by in what's called 'Societies Norm'
Looking for a sign or signal to help us along and conform

We all need markers to act as a series of signposts and guidelines
Humans need there a framework and rules to minimise confines
Barriers get put down to keep our own paths true, not to get lost
Problems arise when we're all doing this and often lines get crossed

Life becomes like the bowl of soup a 'sticky mess of confusion'
With flailing arms we battle on and end up getting a contusion
So, why do we at all societies' levels regularly reinvent the wheel?
Why not join our 'life's train' share our tracks, to me that's real

Being labelled, ignored or stereotyped are barriers that derail
Not knowing where to go for correct advice can make points fail
Being looked upon as a problem is the problem, remove that barrier
Let us join our trains once in a while to become life haulage carrier

Able bodied or disabled? What's your race, gender, colour or creed?
Doesn't matter, let's join our knowledge together and plant a seed
Help remove that barrier of ignorance that bars us from sharing
Open up your world to other groups to value, not start comparing

Lack of detail breeds assumption and ignorance. How to breach?
We all have the tools at each and every level to reach out to teach
Working hand in hand with all this, is a skill that has to glisten
Become the pupil, try and put yourself in their shoes, now listen

Hate Pain

The importance of keeping fit has always been there, never some whim
You must don track suit of sorts, look the part, all to go and see gym
Some folk even have their own gym as home, gathering dust in the loft
There are countless keep fit tapes and DVD's making you look soft

Then you get these countless diets you can get to help shed the pounds
With some diets you do nothing but count with pocket shedding pounds
Get the right balance of foodstuffs, as advised under medical supervision
Especially when you get up in the morning look at yourself 20-20 vision

All these good well-intended advice if fired at you from every direction
Each bit of advice meant to be better than the next well I say insurrection
All this 'no pain no gain' rubbish makes me laugh, who are they kidding
You try to get on with life whilst for your attention they're bidding

ENOUGH already; hold it, cease, stop, the end, finish it, that's finally it
We all have plenty to think about our loved ones work, health keeping fit!
The thing that gets me is this that phrase they troop out no pain no gain
Well I've got Parkinson's and no matter what I try, I still hate pain

Circle of Life

Work to progress
Progress to work
Work; be a player
Players; more choices
Choices lead to 'enabled
Enabled access to a society
Societies we have
Have to label?
Label; I'm not for sale
Sail towards your choices
Choices that enable
Enable regardless; it's your right
Right now society needs you
You need to harvest appreciation
Appreciation for our fellow man
Man needs to embrace a 'need to change'
Change is a process to work

Parky His Son and Me

Parky his son and me we were like the three musketeers; what a team.
We did the lot as one; chatted up the girls, got high, fell in a stream.
For a laugh after a drunken binge, we slid down a hill on a metal tray.
We broke a few bones, no more musketeers, once legend now history.

Once recovered went our separate ways, down our chosen pathway.
Over the years we had gone mainstream, life was more than okay.
After a while I wondered, just what had become of Parky and his son.
Placed an 'add' in the paper to bring us together for that big reunion.

A few days later I got a call from Parky; we sorted a meet; in a wine bar.
I was early; I sat in the window gazed absently at each passing car.
Time passed; I glanced at my watch; they were running a little late.
Lifting my glass of red; I drank; went to lift food from a china plate.

Caught sight of this classy car; parking in the disabled parking bay.
Out got these two guys; they looked familiar; the youngest did sway.
I began to take notice at these two; they walked slowly toward the bar
They saw me; waved; said that I'd looked obtuse I was told soon after

In walked Parky and his son, he was 60 and his son was now just 44.
I tried not to; couldn't stop staring at this guy; one of the lads before.
Both sets of limbs moved; like a tap dancer in a never ending routine.
We sat there transfixed; nobody else existed; I needed more red wine.

This was my mate; the same age as me; how and what should I say?
He came to my rescue explaining, he had 'Early onset Parkinson's', eh!
The floodgates opened; we talked for hours; my eyes filled with tears.
Had we changed? Time had maybe, but we're still the three musketeers.

Shallow Waters Go Deep

Just when I think I have rested control from the 'Parkinson Grasp'
Emotions receive a jolt from behind snared by a net tied off with a clasp
Boulders that had held fast strengthening my defences begin to crack
Freak storms swell the tide; it tries to drag you down from projected track
Waves grind; emotional shoreline breached; uncertainties swell internally
These shallow waters that go deep into my coping skills; controls eroded
Some of my controls may be under water but I have back up files encoded
With the backup codes I have the blue prints for ramparts to be rebuilt
There are systems in place to bolster defences backing me to the hilt
Great benefit has been derived by me from thinking outside the box
The waters that ran deep is now being forced shallow by oversized rocks
As Parkinson's waves continue to bombard the defences water will seep
As long as I have the systems to force back the diseases intended hold
Sorry Mr Parkinson your efforts to control will have to stay out in the cold

Nineteen

In 2005 my body seemed like any other persons, but it wasn't.
Inside, different in many ways, controlled by a number of pills
My insides functioned like any other early 2005; no medication.
By 2007 the average number of tablets stood at nineteen,
I was, in 2007, taking so many tablets I could almost rattle

The pills started the fight in their first few weeks; it continues today; fifteen miles east of Eccles. My body's cells were not sure what was going on. My brain wasn't what had hit it where it was going let alone what was going on (Brain's Voice). How could I cope with nineteen pills? Going from one in 2005 up to nineteen in 2007!

In my body there wasn't a standard length of time each dosage lasted. If I was lucky each doses an average of just about just four hours. Sleep is fast becoming a luxury. Steadily all my cells are being starved of dopamine little by little every day. More and more areas of my body need help, even blood circulation; more pills?

Daily I'm facing a heavy barrage. My system provides heavy resistance to the onslaught of Parkinson's, many loose. Since starting to take My first tablets the body's organs have still been affected by the condition more and more. There is no way of knowing just how many of these cells will end up being destroyed.

My consultants conclusions are that the greater the length of time my body is exposed to the symptoms the greater the Intake of medication or chance of operation. All their help is designed to help combat the warring condition in an attempt to control the areas affected to maintain a quality life with control and conviction.

There can only be one outcome of this Parkinson War. My mission is to keep control as long as possible; increase tablet intake; use all and any means at my disposal; control is the key. The battle to influence my mind and soul is tiring; sometime my defences slip. It's a struggle to regain the initiative, up to now I'm able to do.

I try to stay in work, my brain trying to con me, trying to convince me that I can still complete all the tasks I could before. I can't, as each afternoon my body needs to rest. Cellular veterans from the Parkinson War wear down quicker after lack of sleep, having had 16 hours cellular combat. My body gets sent on leave by medical core.

All suffers deserve a hero's welcome because none of them ever gave Parkinson's any degree of welcome, none of them, none of them. Parkinson's welcome was never extended to sufferers including their families. Just what family and friends go through, seeing what happens to a loved one changing before their eyes!

According to my 'Medical Central' have they determined that my bodies brains messages suffered from what my specialists call

'Lack of dopamine production'. Many cell vets complain of allot of disaffection, anger, or guilt. Why battle isn't it pointless in the end.

Some succumb, raising white flag, to the Parkinson onslaught.

Everybody wants to know "How'd it happened to me that Parkinson got into the systems? What's going on?" People react differently when told of the disease, when walking with a stick, swaying like a drunk. 'Isolation, isolation, isolation'. That's how it can make you feel, labelled and placed in a convenient box, society's shame.

All we want to do is to have control of our destiny, treated with respect. All we want to do is to be enabled just as much as the next person. No matter what happens and how frightening it becomes

Tablets, therapy, or operations bring it on. No matter what Parkinson's brings I'm up for it even if more than nineteen pills.

Air Piano

I gazed down at my hands whist at one day fingers all out of control
Like a line of drunken and disorderly ballerinas released on parole
The erratic movements held my gaze, hypnotically to a random beat
Sat at my computer I watched the show then one pressed the delete

That night I watched a musical competition where they played rock
Contestants paid tribute to heavy metal gods they did not mock
They thrashed out imitations they hammered out tunes on 'Air Guitar'
Like a thunderbolt it hit me why couldn't I turn myself into a star

I looked at my hands, there position and their erratic improvised dance
Could it possibly be, yes I could pass as a piano player at a quick glance
Can't play a note, why couldn't I play 'Air Piano' be a wow at a show?
I could see it now I'm 'world champion', make a living, becoming a pro

I started watching all the famous pianists Oscar Peterson, Les Dawson
I showed my talents to all in showbiz all they said was "I'm sorry son"
Even André Preview questioned the range of notes that I was playing
They are the right notes but not necessarily in the right order, I was saying

Not daunted I took my skills to the people on the street started to busk
I started in Manchester at dawn ending up in Liverpool by dusk
Got spotted by Pete Waterman whilst busking in St Anne's Square
I am now world famous playing 'Air piano' in Wembley Arena

My Dad and I'm Tom (part 1)

Dad, what's all these random things about Parkinson's and Why you?
You have always been fun, helped me along the way and been proud of me
Me who has always been good, ok, and naughty but only sometimes!!
Sometimes when I see you bobbing about like a buoy in a stormy sea
Seeing you move like this makes me sad I'm asking myself, well, why?
Why had MY dad got Parkinson's? Imagining all random things
Things that made me cross, sad, angry pretty much all of the time
Time went by I couldn't think what to think say, or do, so I hit out
Outside I hid behind this hitting being too scared of things uncertain
Uncertain of how I was being robbed of my dad, I thought about it a lot
A lot of the time not knowing how to talk to you about this, though I tried
Tried not to sometimes, but one night before Christmas you came to speak
Speak about how you are going to be or may be, how Mum needs my help
Help, I am only 13 what about me I'm not ready for this, but then you cried
Cried, Dad! , Wow, what to do now? We hugged, father and son, thanks.
Love Tom

Danger of Societies Shackles?

I may not be able to hear as well as you
but how many of you actually try and listen
I may not be able to see as well as you
but how many of you actually use that vision
I may not be able to be as steady on my feet as you
but how many of you get drunk, stagger home and or drive
I may not have the same physical strength as you
but how many of you actually use their strengths
I may not have the same beliefs and values as you
but how many so you have the courage and conviction

You don't need to be able bodied to be enable you to really
listen to your colleagues, friends or neighbours
You don't need to be able bodied to enable you to make sense of all
that goes on around you
You don't need to have full mobility to be equipped to
run your life and provide stability
You don't need full physical or mental capabilities to enable
yourself and those around you
You don't need specific beliefs or values
To equip you to function within communities

So who in society has the right to question?
our communication capabilities
So who in society has the right to say that?
you don't provide the strength and stability to all
So who in society has the right to?
label us in some way within a neat box
So who in society has the right to choose?
Where and when our future lies
So who in society has the right to imprint their
Sets of morals on us, expecting compliance
How do you know whether that door will open,
unless you try the handle? If you try the handle have you not made a choice?
How do you know where the last domino will fall,

once the first is toppled? If you do not know what is around the corner why not take that chance
How do you know a barrier really exists just because
society tells you it does? If you say a barrier exists, then it does.
How do you know whether it is better to answer the question,
or to question the answer? If a question forms on your lips then you already have the answer.
Aren't there are enough barriers forced upon by those that
Demand conformity
Aren't there are enough edits that come from high
That restricts our movements
Aren't there are enough people pulling in different,
Dangerous directions which waists resources
Aren't there are enough people that try to forcibly influence
Our values and morals
There are enough of us; that do listen, that can see, that are stable, that have the strength and conviction to collectively remove the danger of societies shackles
AREN'T THERE?

Sea of Empty Faces

I stumble like a clown amidst a sea of empty faces; amidst of a rushing crowd
"I'm just the same as you"; open your ears; hear my voice for crying out load
Many times I turn around; I glimpse pity aimed at me by meaningless faces
Does mankind need to act like puppets; taught to conform; put through paces

I wish I could see what you can see when you look at me with those eyes
Sometimes you with disapproving eyes; I am still human as are you; yes
Sure I have a disability that necessitates a stick to help my walking ability
Do you wear glasses to sea; Are you diabetic; both make you disabled like me

My involuntary movements can make some feel uneasy; how to cope; unaware
Think about that when your drunk or under influence of drugs; my turn to stare
So you see we share the same human nature and share the same set of blinkers
Between us we don't have to be part of the sea of empty faces; become thinkers

Instead of competing for the moral high gulf stream through heavy rain or fog
Set course for 'Common Land' my significant for discussion, any type of dialog
An old sea captain told me that these waters run calmer; solutions can be found
When those that had fought on opposite sides had discovered common a ground

Shake, Pill, Rattle and Roll

Parkinson's stopped by; a fusion of confusion rained down; what a headache!
Thanks; I almost drowned; Mr P, why's this disease called on me for pity's sake?
Who told you to stop your car; leave your calling card; there's been a mistake
I would like to return your friend 'Shake Y'Body'; his services I wish to forsake

Think of me now; on this new road; jostled by the crowds; left in their wake
Does not this image of my daily life cause any sort of remorse; emotions rake
Why have you not answered my calls or messages? ; remove this poisoned cake
Each slice of this disease I now have to eat; just how much more can I take?

Each day as I awaken; I wait a moment; there it is; up pops the pain and ache
Sometimes it feels you're like a marionette; normal movement; to me it's fake
Full control of me has been confiscated; need more and more pill to retake
Hang on a moment for every yin there is a yang; this poem for you I'll remake

Remake, just refers to a different you; do we not evolve as a person anyway
Retake control of your life as life throws fast balls at you that you have to play
Fake it sometimes; everybody does; it throws the control freaks off the scent
Aches and pains have always been around; fallen off your bike or on a pavement

Take the slices; cut them; can make the disease digestible in a bite sized chunk
Cake is bad for you; include it in a healthy balanced diet; you're not a monk
Rake life in the fire afresh; don't live in a monastery; the future belongs to you
Wake up; despite this disease 'you' still exist; get a new bag of tricks or two

Forsake nothing; why should you; you shake, so; your still packed with ambition
Mistake; we had no choice; so let's shake, pill, rattle and roll; there's a notion
Sake, who's sake; Mr P may have left a duff card, but it's how they're played
Headaches a plenty along the way; win a few tricks; be glad you've stayed

12 weeks to turn a corner!

Oh, I can remember the date as if were yesterday
The day my driving instructor began to pray
It was the day of my eighteenth driving test
He was pulling his hair out and holes in a vest

Even the guy testing me face turned sickly green
He told me the last time I was the worst he'd seen
The broken nose he'd received during the last test date
An emergency stop and being hit by a number plate!

It came to that part of the test, reverse round a corner
We were ready when up came a hearse and mourner
Well that was it; my heart was firmly in my mouth
And all the confidence I'd had went definitely south

The issues I had with driving mirrored my condition
Identified eighteen months ago, started this situation
Body and mind screaming 'mercy' stopped working
Needed to rest, get myself straight and no shirking

It was about twelve weeks ago problems came to a head
My doctor strongly recommended I rest, and so to bed
Day to day life seemed to go slowly or come to a stop
Without a framework my thought processes were slop

With all the lack of sleep my eyes had two set of bags
Tried to force back the sleep by reading some mags
I was so tired I walked around in some type of stupor
To help my brain I grew poetically, a literary trooper

Poetry came flowing out of me like rain in a gutter
I'm driving my wife mad; she thinks I'm a nutter
It took me twelve weeks to turn the corner, and refocus
Readers responded very kindly to my hocus-pocus

My reflective day dream returned to the driving test
My driving instructor and assessor, a state of unrest
The hearse slowed my reverse; I'm no longer a learner
Relief shone as I drove off, crashing around the corner

Wet Face

Sometimes just when you think you've got it sorted, back on top
Your Parkinson's disease creeps up behind you and spirits drop
Momentarily you can't handle it, the symptoms are to complex
You cry out of frustration, my wet face double ply tissue inspects

You try to reflect and find a moment in time that glittered like gold
You're tired of retelling tails to give self a boost, keep demons on hold
But momentarily you feel enriched again as if you're from the Aztec
Suddenly I again feel sadness, my wet face double ply tissue inspects

Parkinson's life some good days those that leave mental scars are bad
You constantly long for happier old self times and scared of the sad
There are times when the muscles their own mind, and always flex
Lack of control makes you cry, my wet face double ply tissue inspects

Then there are times when things go your way with everyone on side
Within embers of the old you glow vividly, the warmth it does provide
Life becomes your favourite coffee blended just right, with two Sweetex
Tears of happiness spill forth, my wet face double ply tissue inspects

Red Cross on My Door

Some comedian has put a red cross on both my doors.
Have I caught the plague that will infect your jaws?
You cannot leave your house unless after it's dark
It will give you more bite that a Great White Shark

The police want to put security tape all around my house.
They want to shake a special powder in one huge dowse.
Suspicions that Parkinson's disease is highly contagious,
And spreads at a rate that is quite simply be outrageous.

As the threat spreads the police are forced to call in the army,
But Parky starts to fight back with the muscles and the leggy.
The development rate is quite prolific; counted in months or years.
The pain levels are reduced with the help of a crate load of beers.

To steady the ship Parkinson brought in a humongous nuke,
To dispel the stories vis-à-vis what it's about, to begin the rebuke.
The condition develops like some dodgy line in a small conga.
The only difference being is that all the effects last allot longer.

Get the white spirit to remove Red Cross; scare off the great white.
Get all the police and army recalled under a cloak of stars at night
The fact I have developed Parkinson's disease is just one single thing
That Parky don't mean a thing if in ain't got that tremor, sorry swing

Word Trigger Memory Churn

Sitting quietly on a deck chair; waves gently kissing the sandy shore;
The sun warms me; breaking down the sun block, I read a 'Daily Bore'.
Children screaming in wild excitement; seller wandering plying soft drinks
All of the above words now bathe your mind, fond memories me thinks!

Millions of minute details filed in your mega-bite memory bank, on snooze
The system waiting for 'hearing' to latch onto a word; initially can confuse
Frantically; at lightning speed memories churn; sifts data; out image pops
Spiritually your back at that 'beach'; sounds and smell onto senses hops

In 2005 I went to my GP over a shake in my hand; like a perpetual wave
Of the causes uttered, I wasn't ready for that word 'Parkinson's' she gave
"I'm not old enough", I said; this huge boulder hit; my life all but downed
Its weight was upon me, crushing my life structure, world tumbles around

My world was forced down by unwanted life changing sets of scary events.
I went back to the small print in 'human being' contract; give recompense
Scanning through in fine detail, of course, the Lord had the very last word
There on the bottom line 'any other changes'; "Come on that's so absurd"

Since that date the Lord has shown me more words; future and hope
Since diagnosis he is using his vision for me to help equip others to cope
He uses my poetic words; maybe a line or the whole poem will conspire
To enable you regain control of life's direction; become 'Poems-2-Inspire'.

Life; Love; Lost Now Found

I met this woman back in eighty-three who just wanted to be with me
She came to love me; married in eighty-five made us both happy
Over the years many spanners have gummed up the works; inevitably
We have worked as a team to cross each bridge using skills and ability

No matter which track we travel we reach the next platform station
Talking things through each time together to attain a new position
Sure we argue sometimes re different solutions, throwing the a piston
We come out the richer for the event talking problems out of isolation

We're driving merrily down life's highway; share driving; changing gear
Tank full; our boys playing in the back; then life hits you up the rear
I look in the mirror and see the name on the van in my mirror; quite clear
'Parkinson's & Son'; I swerve; pull over; "Your stuck mate, have a beer"

With that he staggered down the road laughing; disappeared into a field
Had a devil of a job trying to shift the van, but failed, metal wouldn't yield
This van and the car called 'life' had now become a tangled congealed
Managed, somehow to drive away; engine complained; our fate was sealed

Our love has faced many stiff tests we were spliced; became a single rose
This invasion upon my health has brought weakness from head to my toes
My ability to control some movement reduces; impacts on you; I impose?
All those plans for nought with all the problems that Parkinson's does pose

Just when things were going great life I'm hit with this lifetime changer
Read up about it; saw what I may become; to my former self a stranger
Parkinson's an inevitable and alternating force a total free ranger
Impacting for both, a long term scrambling device a premature danger

I sit in the passenger seat for a while; thinking; I turn; look at the boys
Why should this disease effect them; they look back; smile; play with toys
What sought of Dad would I could I be; the concern and anger it deploys
In my mind I go over my plans; reflect as one by one the disease destroys

We stop the car on a service station next to a field of sheep and a wood
Needed fuel; "Can we have something to eat, please? Mum said we could"
Our food bought; we all sat on a bench in the wood; explain now; I should
We spoke gently to the boys; how'd they realize; it was as clear as mud

Since we first met our love changed from a tiny bud to fragrant flower
With droplets of water to nourish; like a mornings dew; a light shower
But this Parkinson's has placed unknown forces on our sturdy tower
The person you married; I look in the mirror; I see to change every hour

I struggle to come to terms as I disappear under waves of inevitability
Awash with despair with my abilities to cope with the basics like agility
I seek support; a rescue; you are their; giving; I learn about my disability
All is not lost; overall goals are still their; adapt; not afraid of possibility

Driving around Manchester's the M60, reflecting on choices, a fare range
A tiny car amongst the juggernauts; ideas poor out; choices for a change
Options I thought Parkinson's wouldn't give; this I am finding rather strange
I can still achieve; what, when and how still here; it's just a skill rearrange

Hope courses through my veins as from the depths of despair I rebound
Once again of good cheer I'm able to laugh at the disease; enabling all-round
I will boldly go where know suffer has gone before, with family around
I have an eagerness to grow; Parkinson's and me 'Love; life; Lost now found'

My Dad Does Drugs

I regularly pick up my youngest from school, he's aged around eight.
Like any Dad I wait ages in the playground whilst he talks to a mate
You think nothing of it; father and son walk proudly to the gate
Parents huddle together, like penguins, in a storm that won't abate.

The spectacle of huddled groups means little; until I walk pass
The odd one or two stared at me as if I'd committed a sort of trespass
I felt like a specimen being viewed under a microscopic looking glass.
Was I 'flying low'? Was my bum to big in this? It was all rather crass

As each week passed bye it felt as though I removing out bullet slugs
When I caught a conversation, they said "he's the one that does drugs"
I thought to myself there's a few here who's systems ridding of bugs
Needed a plan to pull back weighted opinions, I might need some tugs

Well, the tide of opinion was against me but I needed to find out why
They had felt that they had earned a right to look down on me and pry
I had a father son chat with my 8 year old; he went red and a little shy
He said "I told them you take drugs, your source and your supply".

It came on me, as we talked, that it'd come from earlier chat we'd had
I explained why I took drugs that they were prescribed. Was I a bad dad?
Should I have told him, he has a right to know, he's an inquisitive lad
Although I could understand why other parents reacted, I was mad

An innocent remark between mates had spread like 'Chinese Whispers'
Each altering the truth, sentence passed, the judge returned to chambers
Okay! I thought, right, I'm going to be a Phoenix rising from the embers
I spoke to the parents about my condition, let's hope each remembers

Whenever I pick up my son I talk with him about 'meds', which is best
It gets a bit competitive, who takes the most, and it's become quite a contest
Like we in the 'Tour de France' each want the leaders 'Yellow Vest'
"Stop", I say, "we each have crosses to bear let's give competing a rest"

We still can't help ourselves as we sit there having a restaurant meal
"I take 16!" one would shout as a dare. Oh the staring eyes you'd feel
"Calm down we're shooting a commercial", I'd say with mirth and zeal
We're great friends now all the rifts have closed up empathy is the seal

I'm Tom and I'm Dad (part 2)

Tom, that night I cried in front of you was the hardest night of my life with you, seeing your face locked in confusion not knowing how to react. How you, your only 13 and here could was me burdening you with emotions that many an adult finds hard to understand. That whole Christmas period must have been one hell of an 'emotional roller coaster'. The excitement of that new Play-station game, the anticipation of waiting for visits from friends, family and Father Christmas. It's hard for me to imagine what goes through a young teenagers head. Seeing his Dad gradually change from this energetic fun loving father to this alternate tired weakening, though fun loving, alternative. Believe me Thomas when you became part of my world I planned on being the best dad any child could want, but when I see me wandering like a drunk down the street, unable to carry weight, walk to far without me having to get you to slow down. Teenagers should be set free, to explore, do loads of cool activities with their dad. What can I offer? I would cut out my Parkinson's if I could, be that energetic Dad I wanted to be, but I can't. My love for you, my son, will never change even when I shout at you. My guidance will always be there when you need it. I don't know what this cursed disease has got in store for me, but believe me when I say that I will always try and be there for you. I will always strain every sinew, every ounce of strength to keep control of me to enable me to be the Dad you always wanted, thanks. Love Dad.

Another One of Me Poems, Sorry Pam

I must be driving them mad at work since the poetry bug bit my bum
My river of creativity has burst its banks its flood defences overcome
I shout "I've got another one of me poems" sending them diving for cover
I pin them down with my poetry it take some days others weeks to recover

A complaint was sent to my boss who hauled me into his office one morning
He said, "Stop bringing in this poetry" and he gave me a verbal warning
So I fixed him with my 'Paddington' stare, he changed colour on his nose
When I hits 'im squarely between the eyes with one of me poems, in 'Pro's'

I'd enjoyed working at that office, cos after that incident I got transferred
You see the boss had become unbalanced so to a hospital she was referred!
A huge party my friends gave me before I left, with only room on the stairs
"You learn how to write poems", they said, gave me a book by Pam Ayres!

Sand Castle

It took eighteen months to accept Parkinson's as part of my persona
A block of time that just seemed surreal as if I wasn't the owner
It's like you're scooping dry sand seeing it slip through your fingers
Millions of tiny moments in time, a haunting memory that lingers

As a child I built my sandcastle with wet sand, bucket and spade
With turrets and walls they were usually tall and very well made
There'd be a moat for water and flags of different shapes and sizes
They were so impressive sometimes that they even won some prizes

Now I have taken my spade, dug a trench, the start of my foundation
That is symbolic of my changing views, building from my situation
I have taken my dry sand and added to the mix some water by the litre
Thrown in some gravel and cement to lay the concrete by the metre

It's taken a long time to re-evaluate my life and accept my condition
Maintain a degree of control and be master of my own direction
My castle for my chosen future is not made of mud, sand or sticks
No wolf will blow down my fortifications that are built with bricks

Release Pictures in Your Mind

This condition of mine has pulled out a cork unleashing its content
Waves of words crashing into the glass like a wave onto a shoreline
Has my Parkinson's unleashed a 'Gene' or left a huge space to rent
Or am I a surfer catching the perfect wave to a future that's sublime

Words that reach the page I find are a powerful medium, a rich source
A multi-speed blend of prose forming the perfect cacophony of flavour
They address your pallet, able to tease the taste buds without remorse
Able to evoke responses, may make you cry out for some sort of saviour

Each line I have tried to stitch together like some world renowned tailor
They're that thousand piece jigsaw you do to stop you wanting to munch
The outfits colour seems to be bright and yet in other light slightly paler
The picture on the box slowly reveals itself, and then it's off for a salad lunch

All my emotions have spilt all over these pages like an abstract art form
Painting a portrait, a rainbow celebrating disability, shades for each
May be they'll shape your thoughts maybe they'll make you heart warm
Pictures in your mind, like they did in mine, help cause a 'barrier breach'

Please enjoy my poetry and I offer them as a portal to a parallel world
The reason you to picked up my book whether you able bodied or disabled
Let my words raise a barrier, be free to roam, a flag in a breeze unfurled
Place my book down and think a while, should society have you labelled?

Take One Thought

Brief, brief memories engraved me
Transitory are memories engraved in me

Fruit for thought must recall this
Brief, brief memories engraved me
Written note to help remember this
Brief, brief memories engraved me
One thought, one note
Some stay, some don't
Memories fall over the abyss

Like forgetting small childhood dreams
Brief, brief memories engraved me
Tossed lightly in soda streams
Brief, brief memories engraved me
Those sips were mine
Images decline
Memories fall over the abyss

Breakdown of my memory cells
Brief, brief memories engraved me
My Parkinson's dwells
Brief, brief memories engraved me
Drugs do me a favour
Steer me through my days
Short term memory fades

I count his blessings from above
Brief, brief memories engraved me
Surrounded by my families love
Brief, brief memories engraved me
My wife, my life
Her love through life
Memories fall over the abyss
Brief, brief memories engraved me
Memories fall over the abyss

Parkinson's on Parade

At my bodies military head quarter's code named 'Message Central'
Its computers had been hacked into by an agent, 'Parkinson's et al'
Determined in his mission to make the whole body become a charade
By disrupting communication lines, putting 'Parkinson's on Parade'

Influencing bodies' movement and speech signals at message central
His initial lines of attack were not focussed, in fact quite experimental
'Agent Parky' determined that his reign's banner, to become unfurled
Parkinson's campaign on my body's battle field changing my world

Parky sent his agents to perceptions HQ, to central controls reception
To see if outside parties views were being influenced in their perception
Would successful agents change views made on my personal abilities
Perhaps by making personal and the outside world become ill at ease

Many an agent's tracking devices found they had initially succeeded
By influencing some, confusing others about thing's that he needed
Shouldn't he be in a wheel chair, if he perceives himself as 'disabled'?
He looks alright and normal, are his accounts both false and fabled

With 'Parkinson's shouldn't his whole body tremor for goodness sake!
To me many of his explanations therefore become ostensibly a fake
Trying to explain his reduced abilities and his lack of his confidence
Thinks he can bring about reactions in me and some kind of influence

Parky's agents soon discovered that things didn't go all their own way
People listened, helped and understood what me and my body did say
They accepted me and disease were here, not being placed in the shade
Parkinson's and me we are walking, nay, we are 'Marching on Parade'

Mind Games

Since I have been diagnosed the existing effects were not just physical.
Confidence in my ability to execute my role weren't only psychological,
I find myself shying from everyday tasks to avoid getting it wrong.
I am at a loss on how to get my old self back, to be once again strong.

Tasks at work, home and every day have become a mountain to climb.
Barriers stop my ability to cope; regain control; develop, time after time
Full of anxiety when barriers show; this emotion I'd rather not have it.
I find myself wanting to walk away; this fills me with much disquiet.

Asking others to do some simple tasks; I am feeling weak and small,
It does sometimes get me down; the person I was has started a fall.
It depresses me that to find that the person I was now sinks internally.
I feel at a loss on how bring me back; to become again essentially me.

My family and friends never shirk with their guidance and support.
They are my network and backstop; I couldn't ask for more I can report.
There are times I sit alone; my mind forces me to heed my council
With help can this Parkinson Mountain be reduced to a small anthill?

My networks are tireless, but don't realize my trials and tribulations.
I've with the Young Parkinson's Network; to whom I send salutations
We're young sufferers who communicate socially swapping a story
Of pills and coping systems all pertinent; non of them contradictory

When there are games being played within your mind it's a big relief
Knowing that there are many in your plight, I get back some self-belief
The YPN is like my backstop, my online supporter and 'Firewall'
Linking to form soft cushions ease your mind and to cross Mt. Tall

Savour Yourself

Savour yourself though Parkinson's does stink
Savour yourself through you hardly slept a wink
When the disease stops by its vital that you think
Savour your savour yourself success is on the brink

Savour yourself though you need to walk with a stick
Savour yourself though some folk treat you old and sick
When the disease stops by don't ever miss a trick
Savour yourself savour yourself with 3 legs you're just as quick

Savour yourself though people fail to see past the condition in me
Savour yourself though I can build a bridge to let them see
When the disease stops by just remember your strategy
Savour yourself savour yourself you can be who you want to be

Savour yourself though you can find it hard to walk about
Savour yourself though in can make you scream and shout
When the disease stops by you must to yourself be devout
Savour yourself savour yourself make a move; it gives you clout

Savour yourself though life sometimes feels full of holes
Savour yourself though pain goes down to your soles
When the disease stops by we all have our roles
Savour yourself savour yourself you can achieve any goals

Savour yourself though what life throws up is challenging
Savour yourself though all this may be frightening
When the disease stops by just remember one thing
Savour yourself savour yourself you can still do anything

Savour yourself though Parkinson's does stink
Savour yourself through you hardly slept a wink
When the disease stops by its vital that you think
Savour your savour yourself success is on the brink

My Part in Winning the 'Ashes'

I had a weird dream I was a cricket ball in the last match of the 'Ashes'
I'd had a heavy night my tongue felt it had received a thousand lashes
The sun was high, breeze light, and crowd expecting a game of vision
They turned their glasses toward England's new bowler Indy Sission

Australia won the toss and decided to bat, suddenly I became Indy
I took the first over with a measured run, conditions were now windy
Ball after ball came thundering in, each ball was duly dispatched
I had to adjust my strategy to cope, new actions were duly hatched

The dream took me behind the stumps right I was in the thick of it
To catch there batsman Parky, was my task and I stuck with it
Each card we played he upped the anti our tactics were trumped
2oth over, the last ball, he went out of his wicket and was stumped

I was now placed in the field to take a catch and keep down each run
The ball comes towards me high in the air, 'catch', blinded by the sun
With both my legs pumpin' I ran towards where the ball should been
It seams my legs had other ideas, calling stumps, and were not seen

The ball hit the ground with a thump, like me following it soon after
That comical effort of mine to catch the ball drew hoots of laughter
The destiny of the Ashes Series had been down to my legs and hand
Fielding at short, fine or long leg, no chance I had no leg to command

The team looked down and out for us, was this the end of the series
The commentary team thought so at the time, those were their theories
Though disappointed the guys got the doctor to help me, to try to fix
Physio worked hard to empower me to rise from the ashes like a Phoenix

I was taught techniques to cope with the change and adjust my gate
Maybe there was still a chance for us to win the 'Ashes' was it to late
I was now batting, last man in, the series destiny at my command
Nicking the ball I ran, the trophy is now sitting firmly in my hand

Mentor or Mentee

Mentor or mentee
Parkinson's in me

Mentee or Mentor
Body sways more

Mentor or mentee
Make me pain free

Mentee or Mentor
Medications more

Mentor or mentee
Tablets free me

Mentee or Mentor
My body is sore

Mentor or mentee
Which is in me?

Mentee or Mentor
Teach them more?

Mentor or mentee
Who teaches me?

Mentee or Mentor
Which am I more?

Mentor or mentee
I am capable of both

Disabled of the Round Table

In days of ye oldie England
When noble-men at the time sat of Arthur's Round Table
There was many a brave Sir Knights
With their noble deeds, which were not fable
Many an adversary was forced to concede
By these nobles as they rode a steed
They were race men apart, of sorts that assumed stature,
A very rare breed indeed

Snapping back to reality was one heck of a jolt
A car in front had came to a halt
My case shot the from front seat and front tyre burst
As I crashed my brand new colt
All my battling with the wheel to control
My steed of steal had proved all for naught
When I came around, my head was banging
I had crashed outside a 'Castle' of sort

Through the mist of my radiator didst curiously appear
A noble gent atop' wheels of steel'
His calming voice reached out in the confusion
"Is there any part of you, you can't feel?"
This angle of mercy had appeared
Through the gathering crowds with masterly swerves
He called for help, moved back the crowds
He managed to calm my panicking nerves

Such heroism from this noble gent reminded me
Of those deeds were once thought fable
I enquired "Whence come you, sir?" His reply
"From the 'Disabled of Round Table'"
"Come sire!" he said "lets not tarry
Please let us tend all wounds and the crash report"
With marshalled help I was transferred
Swiftly to yonder 'castle', a 'Magnificent Court'

Up a ramp through automated portcullis they carried me
Into a state of the art reception
We were well met by Head of Services
Who gave a potted history from the forts inception
Such rich surroundings, every adaptation stretched out
Before me way into the distance
It was a warm and welcoming in its design created
By grateful patients for its existence

I was settled in my quarters and to aid my recovery
They brought this top string quartet
Urbane music born as if atop a gentle breeze
Hypnotically played by the cellist, Yvette
My respect grew when I learning that
She had musically succeeded despite visual impairment
I determined to acquaint myself and learn
Her coping systems my knowledge to augment

I was humbled when I was told
They had existed in the courts at the time of King Arthur
These noblemen and women, heroic deeds
Legendary and set up by the King's wife Martha
They had used their disability as key to scout their kings foe
Before Arthur sent a Knight
All their deeds gave much to muse
That I determined that others with truth should reunite

To aide my modern quest, during my recovery
They helped me set up project 'Reconnect'
To bring all parts of society together
Look at interaction issues with all problems to dissect
I began my talks with
'You can lead a horse to water, but what motivates it to drink?'
Then into feedback groups
Examining disability issues giving perceptions a rethink

To teach and be taught giving equal access
To all layers of society showing each other respect
Take away any inflexible ideas and bias
To impress inside we're the same that's worthy to project
Just like the quartet's urbane music

The project's message should float atop a breeze throughout
A plan conceived and developed together
With targets accountable would give some clout

Each Noble from the 'Disabled of the Round Table'
Passed on all their teachings true
Many of their decedents are helping all in today's society
In the form of 'Break-though'
True there are many groups who champion disability
Covering the cause from a different side
We are all pushing toward the same cause
It makes long term sense that projects were allied

Fully recovered I bade farewell to Nomadic Court
Then perchance spotted a visitors book
It came in volumes, on several rows on a shelf,
Bound in gold leaf, just couldn't resist a little look
It contain testimony of other unfortunate travellers
Who like me benefited from their ministering
Tales of their heroic proportions
How they bring knowledge, that needs applause not whispering

Inspiration

Coming to terms with Parkinson's has been the hardest thing for me
Thoughts crashing round in my head not able to be released, set free
Churned up inside me were raw emotions battering the doors of reality
Being eroded by huge tidal waves, my world become one of uncertainty

The wide open waters on the sea of life I'd mapped on my captains table
Vast weather systems just tore up plans, I drew others as fast as able
My sails were shredded, the helm was gyrating like a child spinning top
Hope of keeping of control went when the main mast broke, I saw it drop

I had to think quickly, rig up some sort of steering device, save all life
Friends and family on board my vessel needed to get out of this strife
They are part of my world, for these angry seas they hadn't signed up
The thought of my disease blowing them off course made me throw up

Straining every sinew I tried to plot a course through each watery barrier
I used my re-gigged steering and trying to control large people carrier
Just as all seemed to be lost a strong beacon of light suddenly appeared
With this one huge test of strength to control, toward this light I steered

Finally I got my vessel back to port put her in dock for repair and refitting
Relieved to be on dry land once again sipping a beer, just quietly sitting
Thinking how it may have been, different outcomes flooded every thought
All these scenarios gushed up inside me, to reach the surface they fort

Putting my shaking hands hovering over computer keys, notes at my side
Winds of change flowed over me as I wrote and typed on that quayside
I was a renewable source of energy, a bottle of wine just losing its cork
Then tumbling out came the first of my poems 'The Taming of the Fork'

Since that day you can me on that quay looking, seaward, for inspiration
Then writing once again about my changed world in quite contemplation
I have surprised myself many a time at the numerous ways at life I look
My poems help straightened my turmoil, to help others I wrote this book

I'm Disabled and Proud!

One of the ways I have handled my condition is by being honest and upfront. Every time I have been asked, "how are you?" I usually answer "fine". What a liar, who am I kidding. I should let them know how lethargic I get and the pain in various parts of my body. Sometimes individuals have thrown it back in my face. Parkinson's and the way it impacts effects all those who have come into my world. I have a choice.

When I am walking down the street with my built in stagger and stiffened left elbow. I must appear like a drunken alcoholic on a midday binge. Even that would be better that the truth. Another reaction is like a 3 card trick. 1) They look at you as if you have some sort of subnormal human. 2) They stare, then comes the strange look. 3) The deviation in the direction they are walking, just to avoid you. As much as this is hurtful it is more endemic of today's society.

I feel a degree of vulnerability when I talk to friends and strangers about your Parkinson's. My soul is proffered on a plate waiting to be given back with sympathy or empathy. My condition becomes a project waiting to be put into action waiting for feedback to be given. Waiting for a response on either stance seems like an eternity. It's the difference between doing a web search on an ordinary modem and an 8 meg broadband connection. Hey, I'm not contagious. I can understand some of the responses; it's a lot of information to take on board.

Medication provides a 'Double Edged Sword'. On the one, my drugs replace the control lost through lack of Dopamine. Confidence returns enabling you to function, planning for your future along with your partner, friends and family. On the other you look like a normal fit and healthy person. When you tell them of your condition they look at you in disbelief. You tell them of the string of the various state support entitlements. In seconds you see the questions forming on there face. Is there really anything wrong with you? Are you just another vampire bleeding the state? Don't Parkinson's sufferers shake, your not? Your not disabled, your not in a wheelchair?

Do you think society ignorant or are disabled people someway at fault? Which side of the argument would your view fall? I say we are all, broadly speaking, in the wrong. It's a battle for perceptions control, being aware and not wanting to be aware. Who will end up holding the upper hand? Parts of society put up the shutters when faced with a break from the perceived norm. This is an instinctive reaction, fight or flight, self-protection. Disability is a threat to them one which challenges their world. Then there are disabled people like myself who keep their disability under raps. This is self-preservation, not wanting to be labelled or to be treated differently to the next person. A stonewall barricade forms around your feelings with the tiniest chinks of light for those we feel safe with.

Am I sometimes guilty of this? Yep! How can both sides begin to understand how each set of opinions and perceptions? If we all sit in our comfort zone? Coming out about your disability is hard, I know. You feel exposed. But, who is going to support the non-disabled wishing to integrate? You! With the help and support of other disabled friends, support organisations and your own network set yourself up as a conduit. Set up your own website, approach community groups and lobby the press. Let them know you're not so different. You have the same skill sets to offer. You can hold your own. We can help each other together to form a world of mutual understanding. Help bring the issues into society.

The Tortoise and Flair, Race

The tortoise and flair were destined to race
Both athletes of sorts! Could they set a pace?
The date of race meet was here and true to fate
Flair was on time Tortoise was very nearly late

He turned up at the tack, with seconds to spare
Tortoise squinted at Flair with a steely stare
The longed-for race began at a sound of a gun
Flair shot off, but Tortoise hand barely begun

The battle was now joined but it was soon clear
Flair would win. Tortoise would end up the rear
Unlike in the story of the Tortoise and the hare
Flair had a conscience for his friend he did care

After three miles he stopped and turned round
His friend Tortoise was nowhere to be found
To help his friend Flair, retraced the same track
He found his friend over half the way back

Both rested as they had a winning task to plan
Its aim to be joint first, zip to the line they can
They found two axels and two sets of wheels
Tortoise attached them to each of his heels

Astride Tortoises back, Flair just held on tight
They raced towards the line like a bird in flight
Once just friends now a self-supporting team
They're a win-win unit see their trophies gleam

Parkinson's sufferers - the moral of this poem
The result of this race, nobody is a know in
You will always have supporters around you
Win trophies, achieve goals; see choices through

"You are the key to realising your true potential"

Parkinson's

Penetrating the human mind that we can't stop
Attempting to succeed with a stutter,
Relatives and friends can be hurt emotionally,
Keeping its distance away from existence,
I feel sorry for those conditioned with Parkinson's,
Nevertheless, if you are a member of my family,
Sleeplessly I think about you, how you feel,
Over and over again I say it in my head,
Never regretting a thought about you,
'

Sorry you're this way and, if you family.........

I love you unconditionally.

© Martin Wood, aged 11

Blues Parkinson's Play

I dream of the times when we dined and danced at the night away
Singing gently to the sweet saxophone, we'd kiss and sway
I take a long swig of my whisky staring at the full dance floor
Take a drag from my cigarette heading straight for the door

Why oh why did I go get it diagnosed that day
It started with a tremor and now she's gone away
Why for my whole life do I have to be alone and pay?
Take my part away in this Blues Parkinson's Play

I remember all that love, life and laughter we once had
I cracked a few jokes, you might laugh; it drove you mad
All the friends that I thought I had have all gone away
Now I sit in our bar, I'm a sad and lonely man every day.

Why oh why did I go get it diagnosed that day
It started with a tremor and now she's gone away
Why for my whole life do I have to be alone and pay?
Take my part away in this Blues Parkinson's Play

Through the haze of my drink I remember my dance with fate
Into the doctors to find out what was going on why I didn't hesitate?
That old lady of mine couldn't understand or cope; why must I pay his toll
That lady has gone away; she's gone away; torn my heart; taken my sole

Why oh why did I go get it diagnosed that day
It started with a tremor and now she's gone away
Why for my whole life do I have to be alone and pay?
Take my part away in this Blues Parkinson's Play

I am here to help you and advise you my melancholy friend
Talk to her, she's scared; life can be greener around the bend
Hasn't your woman always been there though most times for you?
Don't make the same mistakes that I did against my lady true

Why oh why did I go get it diagnosed that day
It started with a tremor and now she's gone away
Why for my whole life do I have to be alone and pay?
Take my part away in this Blues Parkinson's Play

It was at the same old bar half way through the evening, yesterday
Sitting in my usual spot staring at the dance floor bathed in misery
When I caught you smile, crowds faded, as you came toward me
She said, "The man told I'm scared and love you, gave testimony"

Why oh why did I go get it diagnosed that day
It started with a tremor and now she's gone away
Why for my whole life do I have to be alone and pay?
Take my part away in this Blues Parkinson's Play

She answered true; she didn't understand my disease that day?
She panicked; her thoughts spiralled; couldn't cope; ran away
Wants to be by my side for my whole life; help us cope everyday
She said "Now I understand let me be part of this Blues Parkinson's Play"

Sitting down she sat on a stool quietly next to me, held my hand
She said, "Lets take this disease together, I'm here to stay", and
"I am scared I'll loose you; realise what I nearly threw away our history,
From now on we'll make history, were a double act you've got all of me"

We had parted our ways, we've talked, now were here to everyday
All that's happened were just nightmares; that now have gone away
We sat talking 'till late that night then they started to play our tune
There was one part of the play to re-enact; we danced beneath silvery moon

~~~~~~~~~~~~~~~~~~~~~ZZZZZZZzzzzzz
"Wake, my darling, you've been shouting out, those eye's have tears"
As I awoke she her gently stroked my head; said my name; soothing fears
"I'd never leave you, or the children; we're in this together; love is hear always"
We held each other for hours; knew that we'd be together for all of our days

8

Communicate don't alienate
I stipulate we all Integrate
Amalgamate do not separate
I enunciate I'm articulate
Incorporate I shall stipulate
Be considerate and motivate
You segregate I terminate
Assimilate you can't overate
I don't hibernate I reverberate
Communicate how I operate
Open the gate I innovate
I resonate as loud as an average gate
I am not innate I illuminate
If you isolate I'll be in a state
Don't debilitate or I get irate
Contemplate how to stimulate
Don't incapacitate or eliminate
Consulate with all, we'll co-operate
To encapsulate, vital to communicate

Secrets and Dreams

Then life itself thundered past my guard
Conveyed on thorough bred stallion
Making random runs, crisscrossing
On my delicately woven colour rich tapestry
A lovingly created patchwork quilt, my persona

Great swathes of aubergine secrets and tangerine dreams
Haphazardly trampled under unrelenting hooves
Spilling into a polluted cloud of dust
Swirls of turbulence grind nurtured imaginings
Energy spent, shattered aspirations tumble and fall

Feverish repairs to replenish my quilt, guardian of what is me
Hopes, aspirations hidden in the fabric of rich imaginings
New directions, friendships or new love, filaments in the weave
Attempts to reign in my life, meets with limited success
Secrets and dreams painstakingly re-sewn will never be the same

Communicate

Let us communicate, communicate listen to what were all sayin'
I'm in your community, community show me a door, the way in
I may look different, different but I'm still part of the human race
Your just as different, different so lets sit and talk at some place

Move forward, forward everybody is trying to fit, be who we want
Work together, together, patents say "There's no a word such as can't"
We must find a way, find a way to get round a table, make a start
The ability is inside, inside to become friends that's the way to part

May your mark, your mark that is what they say we should be doin'
We just use different words, different words each of us wants a way in
Trouble comes; trouble comes when we're pulling in a multiple way
End this confusion, confusion find channels that are here to stay

Able bodied or disabled, disabled give them access to a level field
Show them respect, respect; see what working together can't yield
No matter your ethic origin, origin give them access to a level field
We all have our beliefs; beliefs see what working together can yield

Let's open our communities, communities then sit, listen and learn
Now it's the time, the time to cross those bridges don't let them burn
Every day, every day society finds a way to block our way, a barrier
Together we can break it down, break it down become a message carrier

Paths, Key, Door

The paths I follow provide no directional clues, I don't take to it so kindly
Stepping stones appearing before me just as I put each foot down, blindly
Life is that mystery novel, when think you know your character, he roams
Perhaps I'm a solvable case for Miss Marple or perhaps Sherlock Holmes

To be able to know what lies ahead, including what's around each corner
Wouldn't it be simpler if this body had built in, its own AA route finder
Yes life might become boring if I recognized to many of my future steps
Wouldn't it save some of the painful discomfort for me, especially my hips

Should I have that inside track on what's coming, a step ahead of others?
My fellow pathfinders are searching like me, my sisters and my brothers
Just because I now have paths reworked to take on board my disability
Directional choices should be given equally, each offered, just like for me

Perhaps its better not to know what's around each corner, a little mystery
Which new door to open is half the fun, do I actually dare turn a key?
My future choices are like a game show prizes some good and some rotten
Audience give me a clue, is this the key to the top door, middle or bottom

Knowing the cause of my tremor, painful muscles and bones gives relief
Accepting my condition my disability has oddly brought back self belief
The path I walk with Parkinson's may not be as straight as it could be
Parkinson's became my key to open up the door to my new opportunity

Alien Inside

It's been a few years now since my space was invaded
Some E.T. being triggered a rouge cell in my head
I did not volunteer to become its host, my brain toast
All I know is that it's an evil little bugger, slowly spreading
Its roots are like red weed choking my communications
Picks parts of my body to destroy receptors, implant its own
Whole areas of inner landscape turn black, baron, and a wasteland
Occasionally spots of resistance sprout up, fight the invader
New nerve trenches get dug and nerve fibre optic pipes lay down
They try to isolate the red choking weed, get through to brain
Sometimes these pipes lasted for weeks others only a few hours
Still the Pill Master, even though it's a loosing battle, fights on
As with all unwanted aliens that invade me, eating at my core
I fight on despite knowing the inevitable, resulting outcome
As muscles weaken, loosing the will to function, still I fight
Mental agility goes from premier to conference league
I will fight to kill the 'red weed' in any way I can
The inevitable will out, and I will die, but I am not going quietly
I will delay in the hope of a treatment, which kills my 'Alien' inside

Urban Space Ship

I am an urban spaceship watch me fly, my space's around on up to the sky
From the outside I wobble and stumble, sometimes I shake and fumble
Within, its still me running around inside, the things going on, what pride
Its like a whole different universe totally free, when I'm controlling me
Sometimes I look all normal from the outside, I'm hiding from hell inside
Then again the gift of humour bursting out, plus superb ideas with clout
I'm not interested in just being labelled, some poor unfortunate disabled
My Parky's fuel rods have knocked directional trim, this ship's on a whim
I've got these power pills to dilute the effect, my life's not quite wrecked
This spaceship is now moving on a different plain, a twisting tilting train
Poems, policy reports, children's stories, they keep coming out in flurries
So no matter what's happening to me, even better is coming, no worries

Unshaven of Urmston

Looking out of my bedroom window one pain filled sleepless night
Expecting to see my Urmston neighbours I saw an unusual sight
Down of our road three or four elephants were being held at bay
By this thunderous snoring that sounded like a donkey's bray

Wiping my face, my hands were sanded by my stubbly face
Hoping to wipe away that hallucination and leave know trace
Slowly opening my eyes, daring to peek and what a menagerie!
The Zebra's and Giraffes played football, refereed by a monkey

Upon retreating behind the curtains, I caught sight of Chester Zoo
I raced to the bathroom to refresh my face and go to the loo
Now relaxed I returned to the bedroom and fell back in shock
There was a snake coiled around the lamp eyeing a male peacock

I gingerly slipped in between the sheets, damn all that gives pain
Go back to sleep, its just a bad dream, tomorrow normal again!!
Sure enough morning came, the sunbeams warmed the interior
Rolled over I saw the snake, wife up tucked inside, looking superior

Blue Horizon

I have been press-ganged and find myself aboard the Royal Navy Galleon, False Bounty. It was a motley crew that I found myself part of. Scraped together like a pile of barnacles hacked from a ships hull. Each barnacle representing the drunken under-classes, an uncut diamond. They only worked together, when driven, as there lives on the 'Bounty's' depended on it.

The Captain has gathered us on the main deck demanding obedience on this voyage for 'Queen and Country'. We're off to seek new lands and make discoveries, expanding and enriching the Sovereign's Empire. I shout rebellion. I didn't ask to sail aboard the Bounty upon the Parkinson Sea. I get the taste of the 'nine tails' for my troubles, in front of ships company.

Storms gather threatening to tear the sails fabric apart. Our course veers in ever changing directions. Can helm ever hope to regain the ship and reach calmer seas? There is a faint cry from high above, in the crow's nest. "Steer 40 degrees starboard" I hear. Each muscle from every hand is now struggling to bring the ship about. Quick solutions must be found to alter the rigging. The mountainous waves threaten to tear us apart. We begin to pray. Suddenly winds ease, "She is turning, she is turning" as one we cry, now a ships company. We are conquering the Parkinson Sea, sailing towards a 'Blue Horizon'

Parkinson's Blues

The tasks that I took for granted are no longer my discretion
Its like going back to school a learning, re-sitting each lesson
Why should i have to relearn skills, come on I've paid my dues
Frustrates my normal actions, my rhythm's given me the blues

My hands, they don't listen to me their tremor is like a shaker
I'm great at parties mixing drinks, professional cocktail maker
To stop my hands from shaking, oh doctor give me some clues
To be able to control them, not happening, it's giving me the blues

My walking takes me this way and that, my body just sways
People stare just as they pass me by, makes me low, always
I must look like I've been on the drink, knocking back the booze
Just let me lay back, relaxing and fill my soul with the blues

Gradually my actions and reactions are doing there goodbyin
All my tablets try to maintain control, Parkinson's they're defyin
Just get so angry inside, knowing the battle I'm going to loose
Could do with a whisky right now to soak up those blues

Used to jive with the best, many times to a sweet, sweet rhythm
My movements can have a mind of their own. What to do with them?
Just don't want to move on this dance floor with these shoes
Why can't I just snap my fingers to the sweet rhythm and blues?

There are times when it hurts all over, its so painful to move
Let alone get up and dance, loose myself in a smooth groove
When your body feels battered, sometimes it's just like one big bruise
Well it's with me forever, oh give me some of that Parkinson's Blues

Dates in Time

My Parkinson's diagnosis threw me a curved ball
Where the ball hit its impact changed us one and all
A few doors of opportunity have opened along the way
That are going to revitalize, enabling me each day
So I thought I should put pen to paper every now and then
Listing all things achievable now and to come up with ten

One should never turn your back on the skills and capability you have always possessed with or without Parkinson's.

Two many times I have seen people with any disability sentence there precondition self to obscurity.

Three is a crowd some say but any number of people can empower you to maintain all your choices.

Four if think smarter (Specific, Measurable, Agreed, Realistic, Time-bound, Enjoyable, Recorded) you can set goals at a pace that suits you.

Five alive – you still have the skills and knowledge that can be developed. Your condition can be your enabler not disabler.

Six teams I have around me I can call upon, e.g. doctor, consultant, immediate family, YPN, PD Society, and friends. You are not alone, reach out; someone is always there to catch you.

Seven is the number of times, in my mind, I have nearly lost the real me I was lucky to have the above. Don't be controlled by your Parkinson's for if you take 'dis' out of disable you get 'able'.

Eight times since diagnosis I have tried something new such as quad biking, horse riding, designing disability policies. Don't put your own barriers up there are enough of those in society.

Nine, just say no to those who wish to label you and hang you on a convenient peg. You are the person who decides where you want to be in society.

Ten pins are what are needed to place your plans and achievable goals in your room or office to motivate and re-enforce your aspirations.

Numbers can be used to put together a set of dates and years
What YOU want to aim for is your choice, your mind it clears
They're your possible dates in time along the space time continuum
Each target date gives alterative paths, your choice will continue some

Dreamless Sleep

Again half awake and I dare not look at the clock not even a peep
Points in time drifting by, like sand through a timer does seep
Both my eyes grow heavy closing, gradually sleep begins to creep
Now closed tighter than a portcullis on some ancient castle keep
Ouch the pain in my back that makes me want to scream and leap
Wide awake once again it I just want to nash my teeth and weep
I shuffle my mind like film maker editing cans from tangled heap
Finally tiredness overtakes me; I find the exit for 'Sleepers Rest'
I here they have a person who can help me; a 'Slumber Therapist'

Ode to You My Bed

No matter what I do I don't spend enough time with you
I stay up late to get real tired; who's up first, guess who?
Are you annoyed I'm hardly ever their; always last in bed
Is it jealousy that I spend more time with house instead?

Aren't I buying you gifts; new pillows and a quilted sheet?
I even got you a soft foam cover to keep you soft and neat
Your springs creek their annoyance when I gently leave
Thinking you won't notice me depart is some what naïve

In early morning I use my finest stealth like technique
Reviewing each step of my route thinking of a new tweak
No matter how many times I try it all becomes absurd
You use coiled springy voice; always getting the last word

Do you not understand that you are my only mistress?
Oh! To spend more than four hours in your warm caress
Feather like touch support; a hammock between trees;
Swinging slowly I go to sleep; rocked by a gentle breeze

Each early morn when unsolicited I open both my eyes
Waking so early every day is a sensation that I despise
The bags under my eyes have their own range of luggage
Smugly sitting there as if they were desired; all the rage

I even get help even counselling from my GP, Doctor M
All these pills/potions; she has given me many of them
They work theoretical magic; sometimes for quite a while
These potions try to wrench me from house; using their guile

I write this ode to you my bed at my keyboard, sitting down
Wishing I lay in your warm caress instead of dressing gown
Being be away from you my love was never my intention
It is because I have a condition needing medical attention

Pillow-Go-Round

Oh my pillow, my pillow why is my love for you so fleeting
Selfishly I ask you to support my head when stars are greeting.
You remain in post until the darts its ray's through a curtains gap,
Or until the alarm sounds bringing another day crashing on my lap.

My body supported by my bed whilst you cradle my head, weary heavy
My faithful employee you remain at your station without even a levy
How you must feel when in I march into the room carrying a new pillow
This new pillow fluffs itself up then it teases you for having gone narrow

So this 'Pillow-go-Round' recycling comes around every month or three
How I must take all the stuffing from you my loving you so fleetingly
I know I seem harsh you dragged feathers and all being forced to walk
I need to change you due to my heavy, restless head, oh and pillows talk

Numerically Speaking

One, two, three; I've got disability
Four, five, six; get positive kicks
Seven, eight, nine; like flowers and wine
It comes in handy that happen to me
Brings both sadness and love fortunately
Being wobbly isn't easy, stick comes in handy
It's that or its casualty, now

One, two, three; Parkinson's got me
Four, five, six; learning and coping is a fix
Seven, eight, nine; with you I get on fine
It comes in handy that happen to me
Brings both sadness and love fortunately
Being wobbly isn't easy, stick comes in handy
It's that or its casualty, now

One, two, three; fall in love with me
Four, five, six; still goy a few tricks
Seven, eight, nine; need a glass of wine
It comes in handy, that happen to me
Brings both sadness and love fortunately
Being wobbly isn't easy, stick comes in handy
It's that or its casualty, now

One, two, three; I'm a man of mistory
Four, five, six; puts our lives in the mix
Seven, eight, nine; were going to get on fine
It comes in handy, that happen to me
Brings both sadness and love fortunately
Being wobbly isn't easy, stick comes in handy
It's that or its casualty, now

24/7

I'm on the move 24/7
Not my idea of heaven
Being forced to dance
In a hypnotic trance
All my muscles flex
Shame about the pecks
Puts strain on random joints
Like muscles scoring points
A never draining battery
Just get it out of me
Oh the energy in this kid
I'm used by the national grid

Disabled and Proud

Stand up and be counted
Become more augmented
Shout out for crying out loud
"I am Disabled and Proud".

The Battle for 'Fork Ridge'

At the 'Taming of the Fork' Lefty had been annoyed with Brain choosing Right
He had wanted to do the writing; sought revenge; Lefty's gone in for the fight
After suffering damage from Parkinson's, Brain had forced Lefty to the table
Peace treaty was signed and a new order was established though he did disable

Lefty would always harbour dreamt of military coupes; he was a terror-wrist
Over the months he laid down his plans; wrote down mercenaries on a list
Every item had to be easily digested and checked down to the last semi-colon
The 'Taming of the Fork' loss was more than he could stomach; revenge was on

From the first battle's end Brain had regrouped; Right had found the finance
The specialist gave those automatic guns, bombs, and mines; make them dance
It felt like being in a Bond Film; being kitted out Q; being a hit with the ladies
Ready for Lefty's next foot step; Brain to be stormed; no ifs' buts or maybes

Lefty assembled his foot soldiers in boot camp; trained by a right set of heals
There skill levels had to be as good as brains; the standard of Navy Seals
Lefty and his secretary, Achilles, were due to attend on the last training day
To witness the graduation, the backbone of his revenge, slip on the discs

Since fighting its rearguard action brain continues to face lefty's combatants
The brain has strengthened his team by forming a crack unit on insurgents
'The Cerebral Parachute Unit'; a crack unit drawn from the original campaign
A unit that could infiltrate Lefty's army ensuring that no more shall he reign

The unit often sent out men to establish advanced cells to lay low; look for signs
A unit was based at 'Fork Ridge', a small hillside just outside 'Hearts', battle lines
From there they would send and return information back to brain's main office
The brain understood it had to be on the ball and rid the problem in a trice

At 3pm last Thursday the warning sirens were sounded; Lefty raiders were seen
They were making for the Ridge via the streets in the suburb, 'Vascular Green'
The combatants; Pulse Ater and Sam Ureye were being lead by Handible Lector
Slowly; using the shadows caused on the chest they crawled near Ear Ally Store

Attacks of Gus, leading spotter, were because Al, Vi and Ollie had set a trapping
A few hundred yards from Ear Ally Store on Cochlea Way; caught them napping
Back up, Corpsl Red and a Private called 'Lungs' were ready to blow them away
The possibilities for the action was becoming a mindfield for Lt.Femoral Artery

Al, Vi and Ollie; breath slowed; the bad guys crept unaware the sortie's doomed
The CPU fired automatic antibodies; forced combatants on roads Doper Mined
Two of them escaped the heavy fire the brain was incensed; nerve links down
The time had come to employ Leber-doper means or Aorta Bomb the town

Handible Lector and Sam Ureye hitched to a renegade faction 'the Germ-in-eight'
Lead by the Bugin8tor, who infected hair follicles and nasal ports to eliminate
The bully from the Mucus Sea and Handible the Mandible had the same vocation
Take the body down bit by bit with the ultimate aim was total body domination

Down the main Arterial Highway; they surged towards the brain and the CPU HQ
Could this be the end of the Cerebral Processing Unit; the glands were in a stew
The stakes grew higher as the renegades spread past the veins; all links sever
Who was going to defeat 'Lefty' and his revenge; who would stand and de-liver

Many millimetres ahead; Colonel Bogie's Squad kept the airways clean and clear
He had three men at Fork Ridge battle compromised the brain; the end near!
Nerves now going down, the resistance operated in tear ducts and root canals
Bogie breathed easier when his men, Al, Vi and Ollie were safe, but had lost pals

The time had come; the Colonel to activate his molar, Sam Ureye, and sword k9
Had Sam bitten off more than he could chew thought Bogie; his life's on the line
His job was to break down Parkinson's molecular structure package underneath
Being carried by Lefty's henchman, Handibal, and contain it in a millionth sheath

His contact was Usoff A Gus, his to introduce a pal of molars, Sinna Mate Plus
To the Mandible, influence him; drag him back to Fork Ridge; he was surplus
They met up on the Duodenal Turnpike at the Gland Motel; they talked all night
'The Package' was broken then disguised Lefty's crow knees end was in sight

The Germ in eight's car assumed a live of its own Sinna had found Brain's way in
The renegades tried to resist the Liber-doper; it was their end they were delayin'
Hearts was now able to open a valve drawn them back; deploy a capillary track
Lefty got news; his latest attack was failing; being weakened; on its way back

Corpsol Red and Private 'Lungs' were ready for them just outside Fork Ridge
They had a stockpile of Aorta Bombs; nerve repair crew ready on a bridge
From their focal point they saw Handibal and Bugina8tor; all hell let loose
'Red' and 'Lungs' knew to use all bombs or the Fork was down the slues

Our hero's drew in there fire then through all aorta bombs in a patterned spray
Thunderous explosions; dust clouds; confusion; silence, they're blown away
Vascular Green was almost destroyed in the Battle for Fork Ridge, veins down
White Cells were sent in to rebuild the suburb, a commercial part of town

Sinna and his mates pressed home the advantage and onto Lefty's front door
But to no avail he'd thrown up a stomach acid curtain, enabled to live once more
Weeks later there was a tremor on a nervous phone line; a chilling warning to all
Lefty had left his calling card and warned; The Ridge is yours; watch others fall

Brain has formed medical partnerships to work 24 hours a day; 7 days a week
To help resist and or discover a miracle cure; the Holy Grail for which we seek
The battles us Parkinson's sufferers have each day are long and hard; moreover
What we do to help brain assert control will help us to achieve; but not forever

Painful Sleep

I get painful sleep
It makes me weep
Bring on the sheep

You've heard me speak
My walking is weak
Solutions I will seek

Hail to all the drugs
The system it debugs
Creeps back like slugs

As I stagger all around
Strangers have frowned
I look like a cheep round

"Can't stab your food"
Left hand has ruled
My mouth just drooled

I rotate forward, stopping
When carrying shopping
Some items start dropping

Sheep, now gone, have failed
Slumber-land boat has sailed
Wilder beast, they now trailed

Pollen caused many a sneeze
Brought me to my knees
Rid me of it now please

Parkinson's it did develop
My brain won't sell up
Plans continue to set up

New horizons come on line
I need a large glass of wine
The whole bottle will do fine

Lucky Me Thanks Mr P

I must be one of the unluckiest diagnosed sufferers
Nobody in my family had been Parkinson's disease
So I need to find out why or how Mr P called on me
Research pointed me toward hay fever, it surprised me
Hay fever sneezed onto the scene when I was aged 6
The sneezing game was tackled by stronger over time
At its peek tissue season was from May to September
As I passed the 44 yr old post it was down to 3 weeks
A few tissue companies going out business, sorry guys
The finger of fate stabbed me in the chest with Mr P
A small portion who follow this pattern develop this
This 'lucky streak' has continues in today percentages
Most people with Parkinson's don't get hallucinations
Guess who does, aw you guessed, yes, I get them
I can't smell anything like; burnt pans; gas leaks
I see people in my peripheral vision that aren't there
I look at dots sometimes that turn into insects
Then there is the music, sweet music with no radio on
Scary, most certainly, but it's become part of my life
These occur as my medications or disease develops
But there is plenty of support for which I'm grateful

God's put me in a......

God's put me in a forest surrounded by a range of broad leaf trees
I am sitting there on rocky outcrop wafted by a stiffening breeze
The trees root my thoughts on where my condition will go from here
Will my mind be freed by both treatment, support and be able to steer

God's put me in a yacht I'm isolated amidst an ocean with nil to see
Without any wind it's difficult to head to port and set myself free
How to communicate with the rest of my body with no clear channel
Will my mind be freed by treatment, like a freshly navigable canal?

God's put me a hydrogen balloon on a round the world solo flight
The horizon stretches out all around blues and greens fill my sight
The balloon has sprung a leak so the basket starts shakily descend
Will my mind be freed by treatment, thus enabling my life to extend?

God's put me in the space shuttle gazing down my earth unfurled
The vast openness of space adds perspective my ever-changing world
My Parkinson's though important is small compared to fellow man
My mind will be free and alter things from a losing to a winning plan

Cross the Crimson Tide

Cross the crimson tide
That snakes, dividing the vale divide
With stories I was plied of hero's who'd death defied
How they'd crossed the crimson tide,
They lied
Deep inside I'd tried
Failed to reach the other side
My demise can't be denied
Body tossed by crimson tide
Cascading down the vale divide
Like a child's toy down playground slide
I cried out in great pain, inside burst outside
Flumes of red shot out as my to be corpse and rocks collide
Free this soul from this corpse boat
That bob's like a cork on crimson tide
Free this soul before the devils hotel is spied
A dark, dark place to reside
Cried my last tears for redemption
Celestial light picked out my bobbing corpse
Heavenly intervention had spied
The devil cried
A hand scraped out the remains of purity from my soul
Joyous tears explode
Tied to a pure white dove, bourn to the apricot white tide
On Gods side
Floating above crimson tide
See me slide up the children's slide
Inside a new body I now reside
Have you the faith to cross the crimson tide
That snakes between the vales divide?

Starlight turns into Daylight

In the bible light passes all understanding
The vision is gives is somewhat commanding
And sometimes tasks are far too demanding
Then the light dawns his love is reminding
As starlight turns into daylight
He shows his vision for me
As daylight turns into starlight
He washes away life's mystery

My world fell apart around me, out of the blue
Questioned his wisdom, why me, give a clue
Been a good Christian, why for this was I due
Then the light dawns his love just right on cue
As starlight turns into daylight
He shows his vision for me
As daylight turns into starlight
He washes away life's mystery

I struggled to come to terms, who planned it
I struck out all over I had not asked for it
Lord can't you just take it away and remand it
Then the light dawns his love he just gives it
As starlight turns into daylight
He shows his vision for me
As daylight turns into starlight
He washes away life's mystery

Now I share the lords vision that he's given me
Empower others to access all parts of society
Help them rediscover a strength for all to see
Then the light dawns his love's given unconditionally
As starlight turns into daylight
He shows his vision for me
As daylight turns into starlight
He washes away life's mystery
As daylight turns into starlight
He washes away life's mystery

Why do Mondays have to come around?

Sitting on top of a hillside all swathed in green
Cool air mops my perspirations I view the scene
My mine drifts off closing the gate on this world
Clouds beneath me, grey, white, tightly curled

This place is a graceful special, on of a kind
A sanctuary where I can free my mind
Like a horse freed from stable to fields
Releasing energy racing on land that yields

Free from all the restraints of societies shackles
A cruel world that just mocks and cackles
I can't be reached as I sore above cloud unfurled
This is my space; I ignore the abuse being hurled

I lay out my thoughts try to make some sense
Taking my time with no fear of recompense
Down there people fail to listen and learn
Not being bothered by anything that's my concern

People are all to keen to intrude upon my time
Problems pile around I get ladders and climb
Getting time for me happens once or twice
But as usual all this comes at quite a price

By the end of the week my bodies one big bruise
I'm all yellow, brown and black, now power no fuse
When Friday comes I'm tired up in a knot
So much so I've gone and lost the plot

My weekend, at last, back at the hillside green
Safe in the bosom of my shimmering tranquil scene
Just when normality has, some how, been found
Why oh why do Mondays have to come around

State of Confusion

Always out of the zone
Too which I'm accident prone
Stability of convention
Doesn't get a mention
Parkinson's has changed all
My mental my physical fall
It's hard to motivate alas
Knowing what will come to pass
Got a wife who has been a treasure
Against her success I measure
My two boys mean allot to me
How can I be that dad I want to be?

State of Confidence

I look in the mirror to see
This guy, is he really me
Middle aged etched on face
Is that youth locked away in a case?
Try to escape, show his hand
Trying to grow, to understand
Did he ask or even say please
I didn't ask for Parkinson's disease
Am I viewed in life?
As good looking, especially my Wife
How can I feel a great success?
When I feel life is such a mess

We Will Dance 'Til Winters End

Loves path is not straight or true
When there are maybes and questions anew
The hard part is answering them, working through
So that instead of one against the world it may be, we two

Our hearts did not ask for cupid's arrow to invade
To set up a true foundation on which love can be made
We will talk, make love, and let our feelings trade
Whatever happens, for us, for this time heaven played?

To have the love of you my Jen, for life, is my dream
To face life's challenges as a pair, part of a team
To love, to have and hold; Oh! How supreme!
So why lord do you test me, tearing me at the seem

Have not my love and I not faced spring and summer season
Grown through tough times without being given a reason
Sometimes in this world there is just know pleasin'
Lord, I'll keep my 'Eden', locked, there aren't any keys in

Unlike many a divorcee who had been tried, then they fail
With my true love there two more seasons to sail
So be gone Parkinson's, be gone, I demand you turn tail
For we will dance 'til winters end, my lady and this male

One April Morn

My Son was born one April morn
At eight pounds plus a Healthy lad
Or so it seemed – despite the fact
That at his birth he had no skull
And he lived life to the full

Many years later he had son,
Parkin(son) was his name.
I felt guilty - as his mum
Was it something that I had done,
When he was in my womb?

I sought assurance from the Doc
But told I was not to blame,
It seemed it was just one of those things
That loife itself decides to bring
Upon the unsuspecting

I can put up with the stutters and tremors,
But why did this happen to him.
I wish, Oh how I wish
I could put up the shutters
But sadly this is not an option

It is hard to foresee what the future may be
As the years go by,
But his Dad and I are with him
Every step of the way,
Trying to give support each day,
Being a listening ear every step pf the way.

© Sheila Kaye Golding

I Believe in You

As children we cried, argued and played together
But I believed in you
As teenagers we shared our thoughts and dreams together
But I believed in you
As young adults although we lived apart, we filled those dreams together
And I believed in you
As parents we recapture our youth and hopes together
And I believed in you
As we slowly age we share life's worries and fate together
I believe in you
For whatever unfurls before us in the scheme of our lives
I will always be there for you standing by your side, together
Because I believe in you
© Alison Wood (Golding) sister

Walkergate'

Me and the misses went regularly for walk before you struck
We'd sit by the river having a picnic, giving bread to a duck
Those hazy lazy summer days seem to be fading more of late
You've put pay to those walks thanks for my crisis, 'Walkergate'

At night when I lay down to sleep think of the gift you gave me
The latch lifts and I pass into dreamland a place where I am free
My dreams can be a bit strange of that there can be no debate
I walked wobbling down this road looking down my legs, a gate!

My dream more unhinged on a scale of 1 to 5, a whole 5-bars
I had to swing down the lane I got strange looks from passing cars
My wife turns up with me, which turned out to be quite fortuitous
We had to cross this field and she was a 'kissing' gate, nice for us

This dream state got stranger by the minute, totally unhinged
My children were little side gates "want to go home" they winged
The dream state was suddenly brought to an end we're all tirin
I woke up my legs feeling stiff they had turned into wrought iron

2 Legs Become 3

I may have three legs now, but I'm not stumped
In athletics I've run, I've leapt and I've jumped
At my son's school sports day I've always tried to win
A solo three legged race I always come first in
I work in the tourism department for the Isle of Man
Running presentations, doing signings when I can
I look like that old Rolf Harris song, you know the one
'Jake the Peg tiddle tiddle pom with me extra leg tiddle tiddle pom'
Some may think that the stick is some kind of trap
But it tees them off that I've improved my golf handicap
At the beach I am really popular, in fact just the ticket
My field position is stumps, when they are short of a wicket
Some may say that I don't have a leg to stand on
I say, 'Ha' I have a multiple choice option
So yes I may have a stick to help keep me stabilised
With all that I'm achieving I continue to be surprised
Next time you see me don't stair or do an about face
Come up to me and lets chat then I'll give you a race

Above the Plimsoll Line

Above my plimsoll line this body is doing fine
Alright for a 47 year old ship
Bald on top and wide at the hip
To all that see me I might look well
Below the plimsoll it is hell
Parkinson's is on a search and deploy
To take out systems and destroy
I cannot smell a gas leak
A bunch of flowers bought last week
My throat muscles are slowly going on strike
Unable to let past small pill or sort of spiky
Sometimes my legs forget the forward motion
How to start up again, ain't got the notion
My memory retention is a bit hit and miss
Some will stay in others I want remember this
Muscles are under attack get some fatigue
My pain level is in a different league
So if I get told 'you do look well'
Think of my plimsoll line, below its hell

Bouncing Back and Forth

My soul is a seaming cricket ball
Hit for runs towards the boundary
I'm stumped, 'how's that' you call
Life isn't a mould made in a foundry

My life is like a game of table tennis
Will I be pinged or will I be ponged
Sometimes problems can be a mennis
Hitting a smash into a future I belonged

My life has the roundness and strength of a car tire
Treading carefully; bouncing on uneven road
Seeking the solutions when circumstances conspire
Support from all with a wide and heavy load

My life can be like a fortnight at Wimbledon
An expensive bowl of strawberries and cream
I'll serve for the set as interferers rambled on
Life is not a bowl of cherries but I'll still dream

My life's is contained within a boxing ring I've found
Punching my opponents to gain the upper hand
Bouncing back and forth until champ I am crowned
Be sure my Parkinson's, my future is still planned

Parkinson's and Me

Parkinson's Disease you know it makes sense!
Why it's in me? What's happening?, hence
I needed to come to terms with it, and how to cope
My family, friends and work mates needed some hope
On how to support or just be there over the years
So that together we can face the sum of our fears

For me, would life provide some sort of recompense
And could it be possible my life would recommence?
When I was diagnosed it blew my being and world apart
In my mind I needed to regroup, give myself a fresh start
My wife has always been there for me, a 'Tower of Strength'
The support from family and friends has known no length

As with any disease it is hard for others to fully understand
Unless they have been through it, to help them I have planned
Talking about my disability and life's cards I had been dealt
Having an open approach to my entire situation, I have felt
It has helped me through this 'door' to facilitate a 'win win'
Now I want to help others and empower them to a new begin'

'I'

I sit
I contemplate
I escape
I look
I listen
I learn
I reflect
I build
I grow
I sew
I reap
I eat
I find
I love
I do
I hide
I hibernate
I die
I share
I give
I live

Whether you're disabled by Parkinson's for example or able bodied,
Regardless of just where you consider your cultural heritage to be,
Now matter whether you consider yourself to be in part of the above,
You need to look after yourself; so I say that 'I' gets the casting vote

Writing

Writing ignites a spark in me
Lighting flames of creativity
Heat warms me to my sole
Gives freedom and control

Words form and pour out of me
As does rain from atop a tree
A steady flow forms into a line
Word line begin to inter-twine

Each line or twine begins to form
I tease them together to reform
Into poems with a turn of phrase
My words flow to the next phase

Personally sourced from inner being
Held within verses; it's me your seeing
Waves of raw feeling lay open; bare
I hope can enable you; help more; share

Don't hide below sailing the 'Creative Sea'
It is wrong to hide; celebrate your disability
Get on the main deck; no more disguises
Be surprised; re-ignite; there are many prizes

To complete nautical miles; loose rope; set sail
Each journey start somewhere with its own tale
No matter which direction you point your compass
You have the right of choice; make it come to pass

Whatever lights those sparks in you
Become as one with your sole; not two
Seek counsel be you're state attorney
Live life is for living; this is your journey

Bridge of Words

When we need to reach out to talk entering a chat room can be an empty place
It reminds me of the isolation that the disabled in society on a daily basis face
As a Parkinson's suffer I have been there, lost in life's challenges all confused
So armed with my pen or lap top I write poems about my feelings being refused

When feeling as if nobody hears me I'm like a lone voice in a male voice choir
I'd run round stamp any of their toes if it helped it would enable me to aspire
Couldn't I hold centre stage with the melodic range in my voice deep and low?
Being honest I could sing to save my life but don't ignore me give me a go

Wrestling back lost controls from this disease is key for Parkinson's sufferers
Respect us enabled us, we're not an alien species, a level pitch please offer us
In my writing and poetry I find a world with freedom, a world at my command
Find that voice on stage or page the world needs you; get up give <u>you</u> a hand

If a chat room works, great, but expand, knock through; more people to listen
For me writing has given me a bridge of words to command, maybe glisten
If you're reading my work now, I thank you; please think; whether aged 1 or 90,
Use your first tongue, enable me to I'll listen to you; a bridge of words is mighty

My Dream Band Played On

Whilst a teenager I had a nightmare, which is vivid to this very day
It's left uninvited testimony in my head, scenes I hesitate to play
There were many groups of people dotted around in different places
Some I could quite clearly recognise whilst others of them had no faces

Each group were divided off by ropes, all the paths were connecting
Walking by, my head was forcibly turned to see visions reflecting
Images flashed of my possible future left me frozen me to the spot
I couldn't break their gaze, were these scenes a sick and twisted plot

Then from a corner, music rose with hypnotic tune setting me free
I turned around toward this band, playing some harmonic melody
I awoke up in a cold sweat still trying to free myself from images
That left me frightened that a future lay behind each rope, like cages

With the benefit of reflection I need not have been scared of the visions
The paths between each group were giving me a choice in my directions
Each set of people who possessed a face were those I had in my life met
Although quite scary all the faceless people were those I'd not met, yet

As my dream band played on I realised it was playing my life's tune
That will continue to play its music until I am a wrinkled old prune
No matter which path I have gone down even now I have a disability
I have found love, friendship and support, for a positive choice for me

Take heart from my dream when life is confusing, gives know clue
Look around you and there you will discover paths you never knew
Bend you ear towards life's tune, when you hear you'll no it's the one
Drawing you toward your new path and 'your' dream band plays on

Poems-2-Inspire

The reading of poetry can inside be the cause of quite a stir
All the many, many things written my mind begins to whir
Words and items whirl in my mind and pictures do form
Those individual forms have created quite a storm

Those points have breached my damn of creativity
Words hover briefly, a hot air balloon defying gravity,
Then, letters tumble down hitting each virgin white page
Sometimes roughed out lines are crossed out in rage

Each newly formed word are like soldiers proud and tall
I welcome each to my 'poetic army', ready for their call
Once given, they invade the vet corners of your mind
Their task to provoke thoughts and images of every kind

If any of my poems you read, manages to reach out,
Suggesting alternative viewpoints, society's norms to flout.
Lets smash 'labels', join myself and others against rule conspire
Turn to your neighbour lift these barriers, write poems-2-inspire

Life; Love; Lost now Found

I met this woman back in eighty-three who just wanted to be with me
She came to love me; married in eighty-five made us both happy
Over the years many spanners have gummed up the works; inevitably
We have worked as a team to cross each bridge using skills and ability

No matter which track we travel we reach the next platform station
Talking things through each time together to attain a new position
Sure we argue sometimes re different solutions, throwing the a piston
We come out the richer for the event talking problems out of isolation

We're driving merrily down life's highway; share driving; changing gear
Tank full; our boys playing in the back; then life hits you up the rear
I look in the mirror and see the name on the van in my mirror; quite clear
'Parkinson's & Son'; I swerve; pull over; "Your stuck mate, have a beer"

With that he staggered down the road laughing; disappeared into a field
Had a devil of a job trying to shift the van, but failed, metal wouldn't yield
This van and the car called 'life' had now become a tangled congealed
Managed, somehow to drive away; engine complained; our fait was sealed

Our love has faced many stiff tests we were spliced; became a single rose
This invasion upon my health has brought weakness from head to my toes
My ability to control some movement reduces; impacts on you; I impose?
All those plans for nought with all the problems that Parkinson's does pose

Just when things were going great life I'm hit with this lifetime changer
Read up about it; saw what I may become; to my former self a stranger
Parkinson's an inevitable and alternating force a total free ranger
Impacting for both, a long term scrambling device a premature ager

I sit in the passenger seat for a while; thinking; I turn; look at the boys
Why should this disease effect them; they look back; smile; play with toys
What sought of Dad would I could I be; the concern and anger it deploys
In my mind I go over my plans; reflect as one by one the disease destroys

We stop the car on a service station next to a field of sheep and a wood
Needed fuel; "Can we have something to eat, please? Mum said we could"
Our food bought; we all sat on a bench in the wood; explain now; I should
We spoke gently to the boys; how'd they realize; it was as clear as mud

Since we first met our love changed from a tiny bud to fragrant flower
With droplets of water to nourish; like a mornings dew; a light shower
But this Parkinson's has placed unknown forces on our sturdy tower
The person you married; I look in the mirror; I see to change every hour

I struggle to come to terms as I disappear under waves of inevitability
Awash with despair with my abilities to cope with the basics like agility
I seek support; a rescue; you are their; giving; I learn about my disability
All is not lost; overall goals are still their; adapt; not afraid of possibility

Driving around Manchester's the M60, reflecting on choices, a fare range
A tiny car amongst the juggernauts; ideas poor out; choices for a change
Options I thought Parkinson's wouldn't give; this I am finding rather strange
I can still achieve; what, when and how still here; it's just a skill rearrange

Hope courses through my veins as from the depths of despair I rebound
Once again of good cheer I'm able to laugh at the disease; enabling all-round
I will boldly go where know suffer has gone before, with family around
I have an eagerness to grow; Parkinson's and me 'Love; life; Lost now found'

3,3,3

Three things that I like about myself
Enabling others, thinking outside the box
And poetry, my mistress.

Three things on which I am 50/50
My Parkinson's, Disease, being able to stay strong
And being solar panelled (bald).

Three things I hate about myself
Being the middle child, not being able to take praise
And communicative abilities

Shades Between

Not everything is black and white
Colours change as dark meets light
Shades change as we journey to the night

The tapestry of life with complicated weave
Tests our skills in attempts to deceive
Colouring our past our future; what to believe

Shadows dance change perspective
Thoughts once plain become reflective
Chance of success is subjective

Blobs of blue, white, red and green
All the shades that lie in between
Change pallet, make it white and clean

Precious Moments

"Life begins at 40"
Read it on a gift card
Said it could be naughty
So I tried very hard
My job was driving me nuts
Wanted control of my steering wheel
Went for a foundation degree
Needed to set my wings free
Without the aid of red bull
Did all my study after my tea
Swan Vesta matches pierced my eye lids
Felt like I'd signed up for 3 degrees
Those precious moments
I hope I don't see you again
Passed my degree at the end of the course
Really enjoyed it, I was really inter-courses
I joined – THE MANAGEMENT
I was a spritely 44
Then some bugger kneecapped me
Blew this future away
Got myself this 'happenin' Parkinson's gig
Spare me a cig
I'm staring at empty beer bottles
Man they plied me with the drugs
Ropinerol, Selegolene
The scene is heavy man
You should see my hallucinations
Those giant bugs!
Far out; whoa; crazy man
I got to draw the line somewhere
Got so many pills, I got shares in Boots
I got so many pills
The NHS comes to me for supplies
I get thank you letters from Gordon Brown
For saving the health service money

Been off sick so many times
My missis gives me so many jobs
I go to work for a rest
Work, gives this body so much pain
24/7 you know what I'm sayin
It's like having your own underground
The trains take the pain
Well I'm three year into this Parky business
My brains turning to Chemical Soup
I am not worried though
I heard that Heinz are interested
They now want 58 varieties
Works put me out to pastures new
Retired me on ill health grounds
Like some poor old stallion
Anyway I'm off now
To shag another mare

Crack in the Curtains

My family have finally fallen to sleep
I hear the gentle snoring and sleep chatter
Waiting for me on the end of my bed sits sleep
I turn my head to look at my wife and smile
Reclined, my eye lids heavily open and shut
Thought stones skim the ripples of conscious mind
Dropping off words and phrases along its path
Damsel flies skip on the waters surface
Each collects a letter, word and phrase in bags

Each container forces sleep to retreat from my bed
Match sticks prop open each eye, words cascade
Moonbeams illuminate my writing pad and pencil
Lifting my head I see an iridescent glow on my notes
I reach for my reading light; hand merges with tableau
The table solidifies as the reading light removes the dark
Slowly I draw myself up leaning against the headboard
Enraptured by beams my vision tracks to a crack in the curtains
Locked onto the moon my eyes were transported into the cool night air

Clouds were washed together by the evening breeze, hiding stars
A crescent moon, like a giants toe nail, illuminates the skies
The thought stones cargo stole into the draws of my memory bank
Suddenly slices of recent past silhouetted against the house opposite
I see pictures of me staggering; racked with pain; laughter
Slides depicting possible futures for me and my Parkinson's disease
It's hard to envisage a future with any degree of certainty

The crack in the curtain offered a slice of possibility of a time yet to be
It occurred to me that these could be's are the same for everyone
I certainly will have to make a few more adjustments to enable me
Who chooses the pathway which provide the goals for my family and me
At a momentary pause in my reflection it dawns on me, yeah it's me
If it wasn't for Parkinson's disease I wouldn't have written my stories
If it wasn't for Parkinson's disease I wouldn't have performed on stage
If it wasn't for Parkinson's disease **you** wouldn't be reading this poem

About the Author

In April 2005 I had an appointment with my brilliant GP, Doctor McGawley after experiencing shakes in my left. I went for some tests to confirm whether it was an 'involuntary tremor' or Parkinson's disease. Guess which option won? When I was diagnosed it was like being dropped down a black hole, looking up and seeing your future disappearing to a tiny dot. This 'new future' voyage I could not have contemplated without the love and support of my wife Jen and my two boys, Tom and Jack.

How could I help others understand how a disabled person feels, who lives life to the max, and has the same right to access all levels in this society? How could I put back some of the benefits that I have gratefully received? That is when I wrote my first poem 'The Taming of the Fork', one sleepless night on holiday with close friends of ours in Ilfracoombe. Since then I have written extensively on my experiences as a Parkinson's sufferer and have had several poems published. This book is the first step along a pathway, the end of which is a tale yet to be written.

Parkinson's disease I have, to my surprise, found more enabling rather than disabling, has surprised me. I have been down to the depths of despair and back. Somehow my condition has made me a 'richer' person by opening me to a new world of possibilities. My disability means that I am not 100% in control of my world, but within my world of writing my words paint pictures. It helps me attempt to make sense of my ever changing world.

Writing colours my world, on a sea of possibilities to write about. I have a new blueprint with a new richer tomorrow for my family.